Exploring American History ①

Reading, Vocabulary, and Test-taking Skills

Phil LeFaivre

Flo Decker

McGraw-Hill ESL/ELT

Exploring American History 1: Reading, Vocabulary, and Test-Taking Skills

Published by McGraw-Hill ESL/ELT, a business unit of the McGraw-Hill Companies, Inc., 1221 Avenue of the Americas, New York, NY 10020. Copyright © 2004 by The McGraw-Hill Companies, Inc. All rights reserved. No part of this publication may be reproduced or distributed in any form or by any means, or stored in a database or retrieval system, without the prior written consent of The McGraw-Hill Companies, Inc., including, but not limited to, in any network or other electronic storage or transmission, or broadcast for distance learning.

4 5 6 7 8 9 10 QPD 10 9 8
ISBN 13: 978-0-07-285467-1
ISBN 10: 0-07-285467-7

1 2 3 4 5 6 7 8 9 10 QPD 10 9 8 7 6
ISE ISBN 13: 978-0-07-111878-1
ISE ISBN 10: 0-07-111878-0

Editorial director: Tina Carver

Executive editor: Erik Gundersen

Developmental editor: Stephen Handorf

Editorial assistant: David Averbach

Production manager: Juanita Thompson

Photo researcher: Tobi Zausner

Cover design: Four Lakes Colorgraphics Inc.

Interior design: Acento Visual

Art: Wilkinson Studios

Maps: Leap'n Lizards

Art credits: Page 7 © Hulton Archive/Getty Images; Page 16 © Hulton Archive/Getty Images; Page 29 © Hulton Archive/Getty Images; Page 43 © Granger; Page 49 © Bettmann/CORBIS; Page 57 © Hulton Archive/Getty Images; Page 63 © Robert Lindneux/Wollaroc Museum; Page 71 © Granger; Page 85 © Granger; Page 99 © Smithsonian American Art Museum/Art Resource; Page 105 © Bettmann/CORBIS.

Photo credits: Page 1 © Art Resource; Page 3 © David Muench/CORBIS; Page 9 © Lambert/Getty Images; Page 15 © Mario Tama/Getty Images; Page 17 © Mario Tama/Getty Images; Page 21 © Kelly-Mooney Photography/CORBIS; Page 32 © Hulton Archive/Getty Images; Page 35 © Dean Conger/CORBIS; Page 37 © Bettmann/CORBIS; Page 45 © Department of the Treasury, United States Mint; Page 51 © Bettmann/CORBIS; Page 59 © Joe Raedle/Getty Images; Page 65 © Ken Thomas, DeSoto State Park, Fort Payne, AL; Page 72 © CORBIS; Page 77 © Underwood & Underwood/CORBIS; Page 87 © Hulton Archive/Getty Images; Page 91 © Bettmann/CORBIS; Page 93 © Denver Public Library; Page 101 © Stefan Zaklin/Getty Images; Page 106 © Department of the Treasury, United States Mint; Page 107 © Department of the Treasury, United States Mint.

McGraw-Hill

Acknowledgements

The publisher and authors would like to thank the following educational professionals whose comments, reviews, and assistance were instrumental in the development of *Exploring American History:*

Debbie Barshay, *Bridgewater State University* (Bridgewater, MA)

Claire Bonskowski, *Fairfax County Public Schools* (Fairfax, VA)

Greg Keech, *City College of San Francisco, Downtown Campus* (San Francisco, CA)

Maryann Lyons, *Francisco Middle School* (San Francisco, CA)

Sue Nordberg, *Old Orchard Junior High School, School District 68* (Skokie, IL)

Meredith Pike-Baky, *Education Task Force* (Marin County, CA)

Stephen Sloan, *James Monroe High School* (North Hills, CA)

Leslie Eloise Somers, *Miami-Dade County Public Schools* (Miami, FL)

Phil LeFaivre would also like to thank Laurel Mays Ostermeier, *Parkway School District* (St. Louis, MO), for research assistance.

Scope and Sequence

Chapter & Title	Topic	Reading Skill	Academic Vocabulary
1 **The Mystery of the Ancient Pueblo People** *Page 1*	The Ancient Pueblo people build amazing cliff cities in the Four Corners Region of the U.S. Southwest. *8,000 B.C. – 1200 A.D.*	Previewing	**Weather** drought flood hurricane tornado
2 **Ponce de León and the Fountain of Youth** *Page 7*	Spanish explorer Juan Ponce de León searches for the Fountain of Youth in Florida, and discovers the Gulf Stream. *1513 – 1565*	Using Context Clues	**Geography** canal gulf peninsula wetland
Workshop I: Word Power **The Dictionary** • Guide words • Parts of speech • Alphabetical order • Other forms of nouns and verbs • Pronunciation • Definitions *Page 13*			
3 **New York City, the Money Machine** *Page 15*	The Dutch colony of New Amsterdam becomes New York City. *1621 – 1664*	Visualizing	**Work and Workers** customer employee employer wages
4 **The Battles of Lexington and Concord** *Page 21*	The American colonists fight the British in Massachusetts and start the American Revolution. *1775*	Asking Yourself Questions	**Peace and War** feud hostile militia treaty
Workshop II: Test-Taking Strategies **Reading Comprehension Tests** • Skimming • *Practice Test* *Page 27*			

Chapter & Title	Topic	Reading Skill	Academic Vocabulary
5 **The Declaration of Independence** *Page 29*	The Declaration of Independence is written and signed, and the American Revolution is fought. *1776 – 1783*	Noticing the Sequence of Events	**The Right to Vote** ballot candidate citizen issue
6 **Benjamin Banneker: Self-Taught Genius** *Page 35*	Benjamin Banneker, an African-American mathematician, astronomer, and publisher, helps design Washington, D.C. *1753 – 1792*	Noticing Cause and Effect	**The Branches of Government** Congress House of Representatives Senate Supreme Court
Workshop III: Word Power **Prefixes and Suffixes** • Guessing word meanings • Making new words *Page 41*			
7 **Sacagawea and the Path to the Sea** *Page 43*	Sacagawea, a 16-year-old Shoshone girl, helps Meriwether Lewis and William Clark travel through the U.S. Northwest to reach the Pacific Ocean. *1804 – 1805*	Noticing the Sequence of Events	**Geography** canyon desert prairie valley
8 **The Star-Spangled Banner: Our National Anthem** *Page 49*	Francis Scott Key watches a battle against the British in Baltimore Harbor and writes *The Star-Spangled Banner.* *1814*	Making a Personal Connection	**Literature** autobiography biography fiction nonfiction
Workshop IV: Test-Taking Strategies **Vocabulary Tests** • Finding words with similar or opposite meanings • *Practice Test* *Page 55*			

Chapter & Title	Topic	Reading Skill	Academic Vocabulary
9 **Remembering the Alamo** *Page 57*	American settlers fight the Mexican army at the Alamo, and Texas becomes a state. *1836 – 1845*	Noticing Details	**Government** anarchy democracy dictatorship monarchy
10 **The Trail of Tears** *Page 63*	Cherokees and other Native Americans are forced to leave their homes and move to Indian Territory. *1830 – 1839*	Finding the Main Idea	**Courts of Law** accuse defendant jury trial
Workshop V: Word Power **Homophones** • Noticing different spellings for words that are pronounced the same *Page 69*			
11 **Dorothea Dix: Defender of Mentally Ill People** *Page 71*	Dorothea Dix improves the way mentally ill people are treated in the United States. *1841 – 1880*	Finding Main Ideas and Supporting Details	**Health** fever infection vaccinate therapy
12 **Gold Fever Hits California** *Page 77*	Workers find gold near Sacramento and thousands of people rush to California. *1847 – 1850*	Making Inferences	**Geography** continent equator hemisphere pole
Workshop VI: Test-Taking Strategies **Tests with Word Maps** • Recognizing categories • *Practice Test* *Page 83*			

Chapter & Title	Topic	Reading Skill	Academic Vocabulary
13 **Harriet Tubman and the Underground Railroad** *Page 85*	Harriet Tubman, a former slave, returns to the U.S. South to help other slaves escape. *1849 – 1865*	Using Context Clues	**Agriculture** crop harvest irrigate soil
14 **A Railroad Unites a Nation** *Page 91*	Chinese workers help complete the railroad from Omaha, Nebraska, to Sacramento, California. *1862 – 1869*	Separating Facts from Opinions	**Geography** crevice plain plateau ridge
Workshop VII: Word Power **Words with More Than One Meaning** • Noticing multiple meanings of words *Page 97*			
15 **Surrender at Appomattox** *Page 99*	General Lee's Confederate army surrenders to General Grant's Union army to end the Civil War. *1861 – 1865*	Noticing Cause and Effect	**Ending Disagreements** compromise conflict diplomatic negotiate
16 **Lincoln's Assassination** *Page 105*	President Abraham Lincoln is shot and killed during a play. The nation is shocked and saddened. *1865*	Making Inferences	**The Theater** plot script tragedy villain
Workshop VIII: Test-Taking Strategies **Tests with Posters, Signs, and Advertising** • Scanning • *Practice Test* *Page 111*			

Introduction

Exploring American History is a two-book series, that develops students' reading, vocabulary-building, and test-taking skills around compelling topics in U.S. history. In school settings, English-language learners are expected to learn mainstream content in the English language as they are acquiring knowledge of the language itself. *Exploring American History* has been developed to assist learners in this overwhelming task by using controlled vocabulary and grammatical structures and providing extensive language support. Engaging historical topics have been selected to give students a general overview of American history. The readings are written in a comprehensible narrative format and supported by artwork that enables students to visualize specific artifacts, geographical locations, events, and modern-day connections. As students are introduced to historical concepts they are taught vocabulary, reading comprehension skills and strategies, and test-taking skills. The books thus serve as an on-ramp to the academic language skills needed in an American classroom.

Components

The complete *Exploring American History* program includes the following components:

- Student Book 1 (prehistory – 1865), high beginning
- Student Book 2 (1892 – present), low intermediate
- Teacher's Manuals 1 and 2, featuring:
    - Chapter quizzes
    - Answer keys to exercises and quizzes
- Audiocassette/CD 1 and 2 with recordings of all reading passages

Each Student Book contains 16 six-page chapters designed to help students improve their reading comprehension and vocabulary building skills. The readings in each chapter are 400–440 words long. In addition, there are eight two-page Workshops that help students increase their word power and improve their test-taking skills. The two-page Workshops appear after each even-numbered chapter. At the end of each book are a full glossary and pronunciation key for target vocabulary, a skills index, and answers to practice tests. Each book also includes on the inside back cover a full-color historical map of the United States showing all places mentioned in the text.

Guide to Exploring American History

Chapter Opening Art
Photos and art reproductions introduce students visually to the topic of the reading.

Get Ready to Read
1. Topics for small group discussions enable students to interact with classmates as they activate their background knowledge.
2. Students make a prediction about information they will find in the reading.

Audiocassette/CD Icon
Recordings of each reading selection assist students with an aural/oral learning style preference.

Map Icon
This icon in the margin indicates that a place name in the reading appears on the U.S. map on the inside back cover of the book.

Key Vocabulary Items
Six words in each reading are highlighted with bold-faced type. Students study these in the *Build Your Vocabulary* activity.

Artwork
Maps, photos, and illustrations provide visual aids. These graphics facilitate reading comprehension.

Numbered Lines
Every fifth line is numbered for easy reference.

CHAPTER

7

Sacagawea leads Meriwether Lewis and William Clark over the mountains.

Sacagawea and the Path to the Sea

Reading Skill:
Noticing the Sequence of Events

Expand Your Vocabulary:
Geography

Get Ready to Read

1. Have you ever needed someone to help you out of a difficult situation? What did the person do? Why couldn't you help yourself?
   _____
   _____

2. The explorers in the picture must cross the mountains. List two problems they will have to solve. How could someone help them?
   _____
   _____

🎧 Sacagawea and the Path to the Sea

In May 1804, a group of 40 **courageous** men left Saint Louis, Missouri, on an amazing and dangerous trip. They were going to travel thousands of miles searching for a path from the Mississippi River, in the middle of the country, to the Pacific Ocean. No one knew then that a 16-year-old girl and
5 her baby were going to help them.

In 1804, people in the United States did not know much about the land and the people west of the Mississippi River. The Europeans who were before told amazing stories of unusual people, strange animals, and powerful rivers. President Thomas Jefferson asked Meriwether Lewis and William Clark
10 to **assemble** a group of men and find out what was really there.

Lewis and Clark's route from Saint Louis, Missouri, to the Pacific Ocean

The trip was difficult from the start. The men worked hard to push the boats against the strong river current. They hunted for food every day. It was not easy to keep their gunpowder and equipment dry. Worst of all, they were afraid that hostile enemies might attack and kill them.
15 In November, the men built a camp near a Native American village. Here they met a French trader, and his wife, Sacagawea /ˌsækədʒəˈwia/. Sacagawea was born in the Shoshone /ʃoʊˈʃoʊni/ tribe, a group of Native Americans in the Northwest. But an enemy tribe **captured** her when she was 12 years old. She could now speak several Native American languages. So
20 Lewis and Clark invited Sacagawea, her husband, and their new baby son to join them.

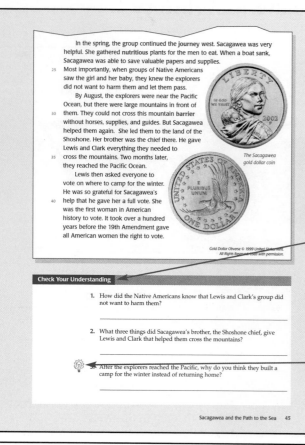

In the spring, the group continued the **journey** west. Sacagawea was very helpful. She gathered **nutritious** plants for the men to eat. When a boat sank, Sacagawea was able to save valuable papers and supplies.

25 Most importantly, when groups of Native Americans saw the girl and her baby, they knew the explorers did not want to harm them and let them pass.

By August, the explorers were near the Pacific Ocean, but there were large mountains in front of
30 them. They could not cross this mountain **barrier** without horses, supplies, and guides. But Sacagawea helped them again. She led them to the land of the Shoshone. Her brother was the chief there. He gave Lewis and Clark everything they needed to
35 cross the mountains. Two months later, they reached the Pacific Ocean.

Lewis then asked everyone to vote on where to camp for the winter. He was so grateful for Sacagawea's
40 help that he gave her a full vote. She was the first woman in American history to vote. It took over a hundred years before the 19th Amendment gave all American women the right to vote.

The Sacagawea gold dollar coin

Gold Dollar Obverse © 1999 United States Mint. All Rights Reserved. Used with permission.

Check Your Understanding

1. How did the Native Americans know that Lewis and Clark's group did not want to harm them?

_____

2. What three things did Sacagawea's brother, the Shoshone chief, give Lewis and Clark that helped them cross the mountains?

_____

3. After the explorers reached the Pacific, why do you think they built a camp for the winter instead of returning home?

_____

Sacagawea and the Path to the Sea   45

Check Your Understanding
These questions provide students with an opportunity to assess their own understanding of the reading.

Light Bulb Icon
This icon indicates that the question requires a higher degree of critical thinking, inference, or analysis.

Build Your Vocabulary

What is the meaning of each word in blue? Fill in the correct bubble.

1. In May 1804, a group of 40 courageous men left Saint Louis, Missouri, on an amazing and dangerous trip.
   - Ⓐ young
   - Ⓒ brave
   - Ⓑ strong
   - Ⓓ foolish

2. President Thomas Jefferson asked Meriwether Lewis and William Clark to assemble a group of men and find out what was really there.
   - Ⓐ chase away
   - Ⓒ frighten
   - Ⓑ praise
   - Ⓓ put together

3. Sacagawea was born in the Shoshone tribe, a group of Native Americans in the Northwest. But an enemy tribe captured her when she was 12 years old.
   - Ⓐ admired her
   - Ⓒ set her free
   - Ⓑ took her as a prisoner
   - Ⓓ taught her

4. In the spring, the group continued the journey west.
   - Ⓐ long trip
   - Ⓒ ride
   - Ⓑ search
   - Ⓓ battle

5. Sacagawea was very helpful. She gathered nutritious plants for the men to eat.
   - Ⓐ unusual
   - Ⓒ healthy
   - Ⓑ delicious
   - Ⓓ tall

6. By August, the explorers were near the Pacific Ocean, but there were large mountains in front of them. They could not cross this mountain barrier without horses, supplies, and guides.
   - Ⓐ place where supplies are kept
   - Ⓒ something that blocks your way
   - Ⓑ hidden path through a mountain
   - Ⓓ enemy attack

46 Chapter 7

Build Your Vocabulary
Each of the six bold-faced words from the reading are included in this activity.

Excerpts from the Reading
Relevant parts of the reading are reprinted here to provide context clues.

Multiple Choice Responses
This activity models a standardized-test format to familiarize students with the concept of "bubbling in" their test answers.

Improve Your Reading Skills
Each chapter teaches a specific reading skill.

Definition of the Reading Skill or Strategy
A brief description of the skill or strategy is provided with examples for further clarification.

Application
Material used in the exercises is directly from or based on the reading selection to ensure that the vocabulary is familiar to the students.

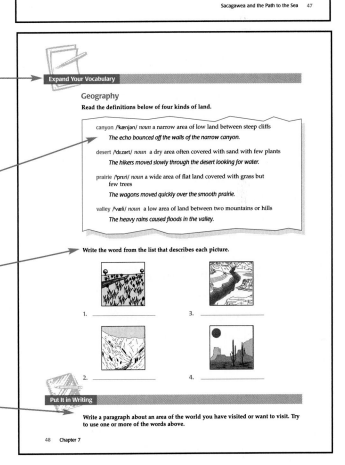

Noticing the Sequence of Events

As you read, notice the *sequence of events*, or order in which things happen. Sometimes the writer will tell the date or time of an event. Words such as *then, next, later,* and *afterwards* can also help you follow the sequence of events. For example:

> *In November,* the men built a camp in a Native American village… *In the spring,* the group continued the journey west.

These events from *Sacagawea and the Path to the Sea* are not in order. Recopy the sentences in the correct order to form a paragraph. The first one has been done for you.

- Then the Shoshone chief gave the explorers what they needed to cross the mountains.
- Several months later, Sacagawea joined the group.
- Finally, Lewis and Clark reached the Pacific Ocean.
- ~~The explorers left Saint Louis in May 1804.~~
- Later on, Sacagawea saved valuable papers and supplies when a boat sank.

The explorers left Saint Louis in May 1804.

Expand Your Vocabulary
Four additional academic vocabulary items are taught on this page.
The four words are thematically connected to the reading and help expand students' vocabulary.

Definitions
This section models a dictionary excerpt giving pronunciation, a definition, and a sample sentence.

Application
A brief exercise provides an opportunity for students to use the new vocabulary word.

Put It in Writing
A writing topic is given to provide students with an authentic purpose for using some of the chapter vocabulary.

Geography

Read the definitions below of four kinds of land.

canyon /ˈkænjən/ *noun* a narrow area of low land between steep cliffs
The echo bounced off the walls of the narrow canyon.

desert /ˈdɛzərt/ *noun* a dry area often covered with sand with few plants
The hikers moved slowly through the desert looking for water.

prairie /ˈprɛri/ *noun* a wide area of flat land covered with grass but few trees
The wagons moved quickly over the smooth prairie.

valley /ˈvæli/ *noun* a low area of land between two mountains or hills
The heavy rains caused floods in the valley.

Write the word from the list that describes each picture.

1. _____   3. _____

2. _____   4. _____

Write a paragraph about an area of the world you have visited or want to visit. Try to use one or more of the words above.

Tips for the Teacher

Get Ready to Read

The first question in each *Get Ready to Read* activity activates students' background knowledge—a critical factor in developing their ability to comprehend a reading passage. Whenever possible, have students discuss their answers in small groups. This gives students an authentic purpose for listening and speaking, while helping them extend their ideas in an environment that is less threatening than a class-wide discussion. The second question asks students to make predictions about what they will be reading. Be careful not to stress the accuracy of the prediction—the purpose is to give students a focus as they read.

The first chapter of each book includes a previewing activity, which allows students to discover the organizational pattern of the chapter. Repeat this activity at the beginning of subsequent chapters until students have internalized the chapter components. This will help them feel more confident as they proceed through the book.

You might also like to have students practice skimming and scanning skills before reading. To practice *scanning*, give students one minute to look through the reading and circle all the dates or proper nouns. To practice *skimming*, allow students to read the *Check Your Understanding* questions at the end of the reading. Then give them five minutes to quickly skim through the reading to look for the answers. Follow this with a more careful reading.

Reading

Play the audiocassette or CD as the students read the words silently in their Student Books. This will enable them to hear how the words are pronounced and grouped by a native English speaker. In addition, this will force the students to progress through the entire passage without worrying about the meaning of individual words. If possible, do not stop the cassette or CD to answer questions because it will interrupt the flow of the passage. After the students have heard the entire passage, the audio can be used in smaller segments as needed. Students can then discuss each section within a small group before proceeding to the next segment.

Check Your Understanding

These questions should not be treated as a test but as a self-assessment tool or an invitation to students to explore the reading more thoroughly. Have students work alone or with a partner as they revisit the reading to locate the answers.

Build Your Vocabulary

Students may work in pairs or small groups to discuss the information as they choose the correct meaning for each word. This activity should not be treated as a vocabulary test since students need time to learn the vocabulary before being tested. The use of context clues is explicitly taught and practiced in Chapters 2 and 13. However, it is recommended that you encourage students to use these techniques in each chapter.

Improve Your Reading Skills

Language learners' tendency to read word by word complicates their ability to comprehend a reading. To help students break this habit and become more effective readers, *Exploring American History* teaches them to interact with each passage by visualizing the passage in their minds, questioning it as they read, and making personal connections to it. These specific strategies are each presented only once in each of the Student Books. However, it is suggested you model these strategies with each reading passage until you feel confident that your students demonstrate the ability to proceed independently.

Expand Your Vocabulary

Students should read the dictionary entries first. You can model pronunciations. Then have students work with a partner or in small groups to discuss their choices in the application exercises.

Put it in Writing

This activity is designed to give students production practice and tie together what they have learned. When reading the first drafts of students' paragraphs, focus on the content of their paragraph and the use of vocabulary, not on the grammatical form.

Workshops

Word Power Workshops give students a chance to explore aspects of the English language that are not dealt with in the readings. These activities can be done alone, in pairs, in small groups, or as homework, according to what you feel is most appropriate. *Test-Taking Strategies Workshop*s introduce students to a variety of standardized test types that they are likely to encounter. Have students complete the sample questions and discuss the answers as a class before completing the practice tests on their own. Answers to these tests can be found on page 119.

To the Student

Welcome to *Exploring American History*. Before you begin to use this book, it's a good idea to get to know what is in it. Do the following activity to learn about the different parts of your book.

1. Open to the first page of this book. This is the title page. What information can you find on this page? Put a check (✔) next to each thing that you find there:

   _____ The title of the book

   _____ The names of the authors

   _____ The name of the publishing company

   _____ The date the book was published

2. Turn to the Scope and Sequence on pages iv–vii.

   a. How many chapters are in this book? _____

   b. How many pages are in Chapter 8? _____

   c. What page does Chapter 10 begin on? _____

3. The first page of each chapter begins with a large picture. Look at all 16 of them. Choose your favorite. Form groups of two or three and share your ideas.

4 The Glossary begins on page 113. What information is in the Glossary?

   _____

   _____

5. Find the word *patriotic* in the Glossary.

   a. What chapter is it used in? _____

   b. What other information about *patriotic* did you find?

   _____

6. What do you find on the inside back cover? _____

We hope you will enjoy using this book and learning about the history of the United States.

Ancient Pueblo cliff dwellings in Mesa Verde, Colorado

The Mystery of the Ancient Pueblo People

Reading Skill:
Previewing

Expand Your Vocabulary:
Extreme Weather

Get Ready to Read

1. Look at the picture above. List the three ways these buildings are different from the building you live in.

   ① *They had ladders instead of stairs.*

   _____

2. Read the title of this chapter. What is a mystery? What do you think is mysterious about the Ancient Pueblo people?

   _____

   _____

🎧 The Mystery of the Ancient Pueblo People

1   There is a place in the United States called the Four Corners. It is where
the states of Utah, Colorado, Arizona, and New Mexico come together. It
doesn't rain very much there, so the ground is dry and dusty. There are very
few towns in this area. A visitor to this **remote** spot might think that no one
5 could live here. Yet over a thousand years ago, it was the home of the
Ancient Pueblo people. These people were great, but mysterious.

     The cities the Ancient Pueblo people built were unlike all other cities.
The Ancient Pueblo people built their cities in the sides of very large cliffs. To
reach these cities, you had to climb a ladder or use small steps in the cliffs.
10 Thousands of people lived and worked in these cities. Many of the buildings
had hundreds of rooms. Some buildings had tall towers rising high into the
air. The **inhabitants** grew food on the tops of the cliffs. They also made
beautiful pottery and strong baskets.

     You cannot look at these great cities in the cliffs without asking
15 questions. Who were the Ancient Pueblo people? Where did they come from?
Why did they live in the sides of cliffs? Why did they leave?

Map of the Four Corners in the southwest United States

* See the map on the inside back cover for the location of the Four Corners in the United States.

Scientists have studied the tools, arrows, and pottery found in the Four Corners area. This **evidence** suggests that people were there more than 10,000 years ago. This is many years before the Ancient Pueblo people built

20 houses in the cliffs. Around the year 100 A.D., these people stopped moving from place to place and **settled** in several places in the area. About the year 900 A.D., they began building cities in the cliffs. Scientists think they did this to protect themselves from enemies.

The most puzzling question, however, is, Why

25 did the Ancient Pueblo people **abandon** their cities? Why did they move away? Some experts think that it didn't rain for a long time. Without water, the Ancient Pueblo people had to move. Other experts think

30 that the Ancient Pueblo people were not able to grow enough food for the large number of people living there.

In 1906, the U.S. government created Mesa Verde National Park in Colorado. This

35 park **preserves** the history and culture of the Ancient Pueblo people so we can enjoy and learn from them. Today you can climb the ladders and explore these amazing cities. Park officials ask you to take only pictures and leave only footprints.

A piece of Ancient Pueblo pottery

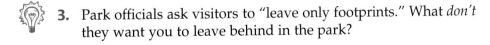

Check Your Understanding

1. Which states does the Four Corners region include?

   Utah, Arizona, _____ , and _____

2. How did the Ancient Pueblo people reach their cities in the cliffs?

   _____

3. Park officials ask visitors to "leave only footprints." What *don't* they want you to leave behind in the park?

   _____

   _____

What is the meaning of each word in blue? Fill in the correct bubble. The first one has been done for you.

1. There are very few towns in this area. It doesn't rain very much there, so the ground is dry and dusty. A visitor to this **remote** spot might think that no one could live here.

   (A) busy   ● far away

   (B) old   (D) warm

2. Some buildings had tall towers rising high into the air. The **inhabitants** grew food on the tops of the cliffs. They also made beautiful pottery and strong baskets.

   (A) people who live there   (C) enemies

   (B) women   (D) parts of a building

3. Scientists have studied the tools, arrows, and pottery found in the Four Corners area. This **evidence** suggests that people were there more than 10,000 years ago.

   (A) region   (C) facts or objects

   (B) accident   (D) type of scientist

4. Around the year 100 A.D., these people stopped moving from place to place and **settled** in several places in the area.

   (A) fought against other people   (C) looked for food

   (B) visited a place for the first time   (D) started living there for a long time

5. Why did the Ancient Pueblo people **abandon** their cities? Why did they move away? Some experts think that it didn't rain for a long time. Without water, the Ancient Pueblo people had to move.

   (A) destroy   (C) make larger

   (B) leave   (D) build

6. This park **preserves** the history and culture of the Ancient Pueblo people so we can enjoy and learn from them. Today you can climb the ladders and explore these amazing cities.

   (A) protects and keeps   (C) covers and hides

   (B) changes   (D) builds

Previewing

It's a good idea to *preview* material you are planning to read. To preview, "skim," the new reading selection or chapter. In other words, look through it, but don't read every word. Instead, look for things that quickly give you ideas of what the reading selection or chapter will be about.

"Preview" this chapter and answer the questions below.

1. Look at the chapter title and the pictures on pages 1–3. What do they tell you about the reading selection?

   The Ancient Pueblo people were mysterious...

   _____

2. How many pages are in this chapter? _____

3. What is the name of the activity before the reading selection on page 1? Why is this activity important?

   _____

4. How many words appear in **blue** in the reading selection on pages 2–3?

   _____

5. What is the name of the activity just after the reading selection on page 3? Why is this activity important?

   _____

   _____

6. Where do the words in the *Build Your Vocabulary* activity on page 4 come from?

   _____

7. How many words are in the *Expand Your Vocabulary* activity on page 6? Do you think that these are easy or difficult words?

   _____

8. What are you asked to do in the final activity of the chapter?

   _____

Remember to preview each chapter in this book *before* you read it. Previewing will help you know what to expect when you read.

Extreme Weather

Read the definitions below of four words for kinds of extreme weather.

 drought /draʊt/ *noun* a long period of time without rain

The farmer did not grow much corn because of the drought.

 flood /flʌd/ *noun* a lot of extra water that covers land that is usually dry

Four days of heavy rain caused a terrible flood.

 hurricane /ˈhɜrɪˌkeɪn/ *noun* a very large tropical storm with heavy rain and strong winds

In October, a large hurricane damaged many homes in Florida.

 tornado /tɔrˈneɪdoʊ/ *noun* a violent storm with strong wind that often comes down from one cloud

The tornado lifted the car into the air.

True or False? Use the definitions. Fill in the correct bubble. The first one has been done for you.

		True	False
1.	Farmers need a drought to grow corn and other vegetables.	ⓣ	●
2.	Floods, hurricanes, and droughts all bring a lot of water.	ⓣ	Ⓕ
3.	Floods and droughts are bad for farmers.	ⓣ	Ⓕ
4.	One tornado probably does more damage than one huricane.	ⓣ	Ⓕ

Write a paragraph about the weather where you live or have lived. Try to use one or more of the words above.

Juan Ponce de León searches for the Fountain of Youth.

Ponce de León and the Fountain of Youth

Reading Skill:
Using Context Clues

Expand Your Vocabulary:
Geography

Get Ready to Read

1. A new energy drink promises to keep you young forever. Will you buy this drink? Give two reasons why you want to stay young forever or why you do not want to.

_____

_____

2. Look at the picture above and read the title of this chapter. Do you think the search for the Fountain of Youth will be easy or hard? Why or why not?

_____

_____

🎧 Ponce de León and the Fountain of Youth

1   Today, it is silly to believe that magic water can keep you young forever. But in 1513 it did seem possible. A few years earlier, explorers came back to Europe with exciting stories about North and South America across the ocean. People in Europe thought that there really could be a fountain of

5   youth and piles of gold in this new place.

Juan Ponce de León, a Spanish explorer, loved adventure. He was so adventurous that he came to the Americas to search for gold and other **treasures**. But he was also sometimes **cruel** and greedy. On the island of Puerto Rico, his army made the native people slaves and stole their treasures.

10   While he was there, he heard **rumors** about a fountain of youth. The native people's stories said this magic fountain was north on the island of Bimini.

In 1513, Ponce de León used the treasures he took from the native people to pay for his next adventure—the search for the Fountain of Youth. On March 3, Ponce de León left Puerto Rico with about 200 men on three

15   ships. He traveled around several islands and searched for Bimini. But he didn't find a magic fountain or piles of gold. Ponce de León **ordered** the captains of his ships to sail north. They quickly followed his directions.

 *

On March 27, 1513, Ponce de León saw the coast of North America for the first time. He named this new place *Florida*. Native people there attacked Ponce

20   de León and his men. These native people stopped Ponce de León and his men from exploring the land. So, finally, they sailed away without searching for the fountain. This time Ponce de León ordered his captains to sail south.

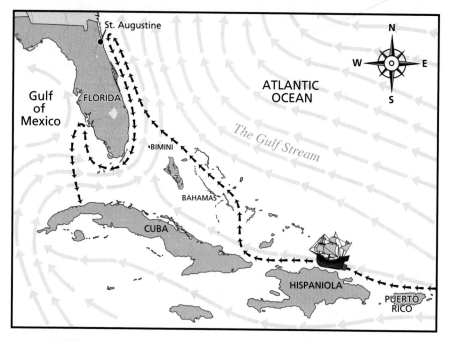

Ponce de Léon's route and the Gulf Stream

---

* See the map on the inside back cover for the location of Florida in the United States.

Then Ponce de León and his men discovered something very important. A powerful ocean **current** was pushing against the ships. The ships could not
25 move south easily, even when strong winds were pushing them in that direction. This is how Ponce de León discovered the Gulf Stream. This strong ocean current flows north along the coast of North America and then turns east. Even today this highway in the sea is an important
30 path for ships sailing to Europe.

Ponce de León never found the Fountain of Youth. In 1521, he was still searching for it when native people attacked and killed him. In 1565, the
35 Spanish settled at a place they named Saint Augustine. This place was near the spot where Ponce de León landed 52 years earlier. The city of St. Augustine, Florida, is still there today. It's the oldest **permanent**
40 settlement in the United States.

The Fountain of Youth Park in Saint Augustine, Florida

Check Your Understanding

1. Where did the native people say the fountain of youth was?

   _____

   _____

2. In the ovals below write three more words or phrases that describe Ponce de León's personality and actions.

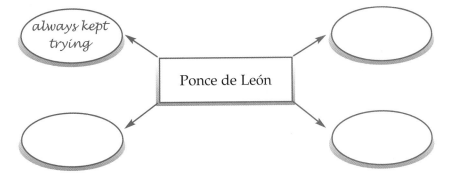

always kept trying

Ponce de León

What is the meaning of each word in blue? Fill in the correct bubble.

1. He was so adventurous that he came to the Americas to search for gold and other **treasures**.

   Ⓐ things that are worth a lot of money
   Ⓑ people living in distant places
   Ⓒ guns and other weapons
   Ⓓ enemies

2. But he was also sometimes **cruel** and greedy. On the island of Puerto Rico, his army made the native people slaves and stole their treasures.

   Ⓐ careful
   Ⓑ brave
   Ⓒ happy
   Ⓓ mean

3. While he was there, he heard **rumors** about a fountain of youth. The native people's stories said this magic fountain was north on the island of Bimini.

   Ⓐ angry statements
   Ⓑ stories that may not be true
   Ⓒ native music
   Ⓓ animal sounds

4. But he didn't find a magic fountain or piles of gold. Ponce de León **ordered** the captains of his ships to sail north. They quickly followed his directions.

   Ⓐ looked for something
   Ⓑ honored someone
   Ⓒ told someone to do something
   Ⓓ asked about something

5. A powerful ocean **current** was pushing against the ships. The ships could not move south easily, even when strong winds were pushing them in that direction.

   Ⓐ large fish
   Ⓑ movement of water
   Ⓒ big rock
   Ⓓ powerful storm

6. The city of Saint Augustine, Florida, is still there today. It's the oldest **permanent** settlement in the United States.

   Ⓐ lasting forever
   Ⓑ modern
   Ⓒ near the ocean
   Ⓓ protected

Using Context Clues

When you don't know a word in a reading selection, use the words and sentences before and after it to help you guess its meaning. These words and sentences are called *context clues*. For example:

> He was so adventurous that he came to the Americas to search for gold and other **treasures**.

The phrase "gold and other treasures" tells you that gold is one kind of treasure. Gold is very valuable. A treasure, therefore, is probably something that is worth a lot of money.

Look at these sentences from the reading again. Underline the words or sentences that help you guess the meaning of the word in blue. The first one has been done for you.

1. But he was also sometimes **cruel** and greedy. On the island of Puerto Rico, his army made the native people slaves and stole their treasures.

2. While he was there, he heard **rumors** about a fountain of youth. The native people's stories said this magic fountain was north on the island of Bimini.

3. Ponce de León **ordered** the captains of his ships to sail north. They quickly followed his directions.

4. A powerful ocean **current** was pushing against the ships. The ships could not move south easily, even when strong winds were pushing them in that direction.

5. The city of Saint Augustine, Florida, is still there today. It's the oldest **permanent** settlement in the United States.

Now look again at your answers to the vocabulary questions on page 10. Change any answers you think are wrong.

Geography

Read the definitions below of four words that name ways in which water and land come together.

canal /kəˈnæl/ *noun* an artificial river for ships

> *The Erie Canal is 360 miles long and took eight years to build.*

gulf /gʌlf/ *noun* a large area of ocean that is partly surrounded by land

> *The storm moved quickly over the warm water of the gulf.*

peninsula /pəˈnɪnsələ/ *noun* a piece of land that sticks out into an area of water

> *The lighthouse was built on a peninsula so passing ships could see it.*

wetland /ˈwɛtˈlænd/ *noun* an area of land that is usually covered by water

> *Laws now protect the wetlands from being destroyed by builders.*

Write the word from above that describes the area in each picture.

1. _____

2. _____

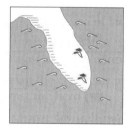

3. _____

4. _____

Write a paragraph about the geography of your town or state and the areas of water in it. If possible, use one or more of the words above.

The Dictionary

Guidewords are at the top of the page and tell you the first and last words on the page.

Words are listed in **alphabetical order**. If the first letters of two words are the same, the second letters of the words are used. If the second letters are the same, the third letters are used.

The **pronunciation** is given after each word. A chart, usually at the front or back of the dictionary, explains how to pronounce each symbol. There is a pronunciation chart in this book on page 113.

The **part of speech** tells you if a word is a verb, noun, adjective, adverb, etc. Knowing this tells you how to use the word in a sentence.

Other forms of nouns and verbs that are irregular or follow special spelling rules are sometimes given.

When there is more than one **definition**, each definition is numbered.

---

horn / hull

horn /hɔrn/ *noun* **1** a hard bone-like growth on the heads of cows, goats, and other animals **2** a musical instrument such as a trumpet or tuba **3** a piece of equipment in a car or other vehicle that can make a warning sound

---

hug /hʌg/ *verb* **hugs, hugged, hugging** to hold someone tightly in your arms **— hug** *noun* an action of holding someone tightly in your arms

---

hull / hʌl/ *noun* **1** the lower body of a ship or plane **2** the outside part of a seed

---

Study the labels for the dictionary sample above. Then fill in the bubble of the correct answer to each question.

1. Which of these words would be found on a dictionary page with the guidewords **camel/celery**?

   Ⓐ cereal   Ⓒ button

   Ⓑ catch   Ⓓ cabbage

2. Which group of words is in alphabetical order?

    Ⓐ brave
        boy
        crow
        dog

    Ⓒ figure
        finger
        fater
        gift

    Ⓑ hungry
        hurry
        metal
        nose

    Ⓓ thumb
        ticket
        stick
        vault

3. Which word on page 13 can be two different parts of speech?

    Ⓐ horn

    Ⓒ hull

    Ⓑ hug

    Ⓓ none

4. Which definition of *horn* on page 13 is used in the sentence below?

    The driver blew his horn to scare the cat out of the street.

    Ⓐ definition 1

    Ⓒ definition 3

    Ⓑ definition 2

    Ⓓ none of these definitions

Look up the word *responsibility* in a classroom dictionary. Then answer these questions.

5. What guidewords are at the top of the page?

    _____

6. What part of speech is *responsibility*? _____

7. How many definitions are given for *responsibility*? _____

8. Are any other forms of *responsibility* given? _____ If so, what

    are they? _____

9. Write a sentence using the word *responsibility*.

    _____

    _____

The island of Manhattan in New York City today

New York City, the Money Machine

Reading Skill:
Visualizing

Expand Your Vocabulary:
Work and Workers

Get Ready to Read

1. List three things you know about New York City.

_____

_____

_____

2. Think about the title of this chapter. Why do you think New York City is called a money machine?

_____

_____

New York City, the Money Machine   15

🎧 New York City, the Money Machine

1   People come to America for many reasons. Some want religious freedom. Others are escaping cruel governments.

5   The first Dutch people in America, however, came from the Netherlands to make money. They came to the area where New York City is today because the land there was full of animals with beautiful furs. They sent the furs across the ocean to Europe in big ships. In Europe they sold the furs for a big **profit**.

The original Dutch fort and trading station of New Amsterdam on the island of Manhattan

In 1621, a group of Dutch **investors** started the Dutch West India

15   Company. It gathered furs and other things in America to sell in Europe. Peter Minuit /ˈmɪnjuɪt/ was the director of the company. He decided to build the main office on an island the Native Americans called Manhattan. Minuit **purchased** the island from the Native Americans for about $24 worth of goods. However, the Native Americans didn't understand that they were selling the island. They

20   believed land could be used but not owned.

Minuit named his trading station *New Amsterdam* for the most important city in the Netherlands. The company built a fort on the southern end of the island and put the company's business office inside. People from many nations lived and worked together there. The trading station was a big

25   success, and the company quickly became **prosperous**.

Great Britain, the Netherlands, and their colonies in the New York area around 1650

* See the map on the inside back cover for the location of New York City in the United States.

British trading stations nearby were not nearly as successful, and the British became **jealous** of the Dutch. The British (people from England, Scotland, and Wales) therefore, became friendly with powerful Native American groups and made agreements with them. This frightened the Dutch. To protect themselves, the Dutch

30 built a wooden wall across the lower part of Manhattan Island. In 1664, the King of England decided that he wanted the Dutch **colony**. So he sent ships of soldiers to take New Amsterdam. The Dutch governor knew the wooden wall was not strong enough, so he simply gave up the island without fighting. The English king gave the colony to his brother, the Duke of York, and renamed it *New York*. Now the

35 British could use the area to make money.

Over the years, the settlement on Manhattan became richer and larger. People took wood from the Dutch wall and used it for firewood. Today New York City is the most important business center in the world. The place where the wall used to be is now a road called *Wall Street*. It is the home of the New York Stock Exchange.

40 Businesspeople from all over the world buy and sell stocks there every day.

The New York Stock Exchange on Wall Street today

Check Your Understanding

True or False? Fill in the correct bubble.

		True	False
💡	**1.** In the 1600s, people in Europe wanted animal furs.	Ⓣ	Ⓕ
	2. The Dutch and the Native Americans had different beliefs about land.	Ⓣ	Ⓕ
	3. A wooden wall kept the British army out of Manhattan for a long time.	Ⓣ	Ⓕ

What is the meaning of each word in blue? Fill in the correct bubble.

1. They sent the furs across the ocean to Europe in big ships. In Europe they sold the furs for a big **profit**.

   (A) money that a business makes   (C) land that a king owns

   (B) warm fur clothing   (D) a place for a lot of supplies

2. In 1621, a group of Dutch **investors** started the Dutch West India Company. It gathered furs and other things in America to sell in Europe.

   (A) members of the Dutch royal family   (C) workers who leave a company

   (B) people who use their money to form a business   (D) people who work for food instead of money

3. Minuit **purchased** the island from the Native Americans for about $24 worth of goods.

   (A) took by force   (C) stole

   (B) bought   (D) wanted

4. The trading station was a big success, and the company quickly became **prosperous**.

   (A) unable to find workers   (C) under attack by enemies
   (B) poor   (D) good at making money

5. British trading stations nearby were not nearly as successful, and the British became **jealous** of the Dutch.

   (A) afraid of being attacked   (C) helpful and caring

   (B) pleased with what you have done   (D) unhappy because you want what someone else has

6. To protect themselves, the Dutch built a wooden wall across the lower part of Manhattan Island. In 1664, the King of England decided that he wanted the Dutch **colony**.

   (A) skilled workers   (C) area that is controlled by a more powerful country

   (B) ship used for carrying goods to Europe   (D) place where supplies are kept

Visualizing

When you read, it is helpful to make pictures in your mind. Try to "see" the people, things, or events the writer is describing. This is called *visualizing*.

1. Reread these sentences from the reading selection. As you read, *visualize* the people and events.

   > The first Dutch people in America, however, came from the Netherlands to make money. They came to the area where New York City is today because the land there was full of animals with beautiful furs. They sent the furs across the ocean to Europe in big ships. In Europe they sold the furs for a big profit.

2. Draw one or more pictures on your own paper showing how you visualized the paragraph.

3. Write the name of each thing under its picture.

4. Now reread these sentences from the reading selection. Visualize what you read.

   > In 1664, the King of England decided that he wanted the Dutch colony. So he sent ships of soldiers to take New Amsterdam. The Dutch governor knew the wooden wall was not strong enough, so he simply gave up the island without fighting.

5. Draw a picture of what you visualized and write the name of each thing you show.

6. Form groups of two or three students. Explain your pictures to other members of your group.

7. Reread the reading selection on pages 16 and 17. Visualize the people, things, and events as you read.

Work and Workers

Read the definitions below of four words that are related to work and workers.

customer /ˈkʌstəmər/ *noun* a person who buys goods or services from a store

The owner greets every customer who enters her store.

employee /ɪmˈplɔɪi/ *noun* a person who is paid to work for another person or company

My father is an employee of the Quality Food Company.

employer /ɪmˈplɔɪər/ *noun* a person or business that pays someone to do work

The tire factory is the largest employer in our town.

wages /ˈweɪdʒəs/ *noun* [plural] money given to a worker for work he or she has done

The work is difficult, but the wages are good.

Look at the picture on the left. Then answer each question.

1. Who is the employer? _____

2. What wages do they pay? _____

3. Who is the employee? _____

4. Who is the customer? Draw a circle around the customer.

Write a paragraph about the work that one of your friends or family members does. Try to use one or more of the words above.

On Patriots' Day these actors dressed as British troops prepare to meet other actors dressed as colonists at North Bridge in Concord, Massachusetts.

The Battles of Lexington and Concord

Reading Skill:
Asking Yourself Questions

Expand Your Vocabulary:
Peace and War

Get Ready to Read

1. Are some things so unfair that people or countries should fight in order to change them? List one and tell why it is important and worth fighting for.

   _____

   _____

2. Look at the picture above and read the title of this chapter. List three questions you think this reading selection will answer.

   _____

   _____

The Battles of Lexington and Concord

1   The people in Boston, Massachusetts, were angry in April 1775. Massachusetts was one of the 13 British **colonies** in America. The **colonists** there were still ruled by the King of England. He was charging very high taxes on everything from tea to paper. Now he ordered them not to have town
5   meetings without the **approval** of his royal governor. The **tension** and bad feelings between the colonists and British soldiers were getting worse every day.

   On the night of April 18, General Gage, the British governor of Massachusetts, heard that colonists were hiding guns in Lexington and Concord, two towns near Boston. He was afraid that they were planning an attack. He
10   decided to send soldiers to Lexington and Concord that night. In the morning, they planned to surprise the colonists and **seize** the guns. However, the colonists found out about the plan and made their own plans.

   While the British troops were getting ready, a colonist named Paul Revere got on his horse and rode off. He wanted to warn the men who were guarding the
15   guns in Lexington and Concord. He left four hours before the British troops. Revere arrived in Lexington early in the morning. When 700 British soldiers arrived later, 70 colonists with guns met them. The British commander ordered the colonists to drop their guns. No one did. For a few seconds, no one moved. Then someone fired a shot. This was followed by hundreds of shots. Ten colonists were
20   killed. This is how the colonists began their **rebellion** against England.

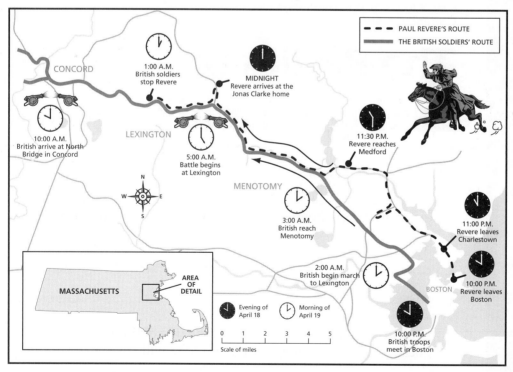

The routes of Paul Revere and the British soldiers from Boston toward Lexington and Concord, Massachusetts

The British commander then ordered his troops to march to Concord. The colonists were ready for them. They met the British troops at Concord's North Bridge. This time the battle ended differently. Many British soldiers were **wounded** or killed and the British army moved back. The colonists
25 chased them all the way back to Boston. This was the beginning of the war between the American colonies and England that is called the American Revolution.

Today, no one knows who fired the first shot at Lexington. In a poem written 62 years later, this shot was called "the shot heard round the world."
30 It showed people around the world that Americans were willing to fight and even die to be free.

In Massachusetts, the third Monday in April is called Patriots' Day. This holiday reminds us of the first battles of the American Revolution. In the morning, actors dress in colonial clothes and repeat Paul Revere's famous
35 ride. The battle is fought again at the North Bridge, but this time it is fought by actors in costumes.

Check Your Understanding

1. Write these four events in the boxes in the order that they happened.

   • British troops returned to Boston.

   • Paul Revere arrived at Lexington.

   • General Gage brought his troops together.

   • British troops arrived at Concord.

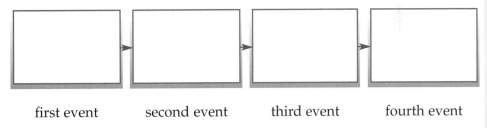

   first event   second event   third event   fourth event

 2. What does it mean that the first shot from this battle was heard around

   the world? _____

   _____

   _____

What is the meaning of each word in blue? Fill in the correct bubble.

1. Massachusetts was one of the 13 British colonies in America. The **colonists** there were still ruled by the king of England.

    (A) skilled workers   (C) people who fight to be free

    (B) people who live in colonies   (D) friends of the king

2. He was charging very high taxes on everything from tea to paper. Now he ordered them not to have town meetings without the **approval** of his royal governor.

    (A) British troops   (C) help

    (B) tax money   (D) permission

3. The **tension** and bad feelings between the colonists and British soldiers were getting worse every day.

    (A) strong friendship   (C) new agreement

    (B) unfriendly feelings and anger   (D) trust

4. He decided to send soldiers to Lexington and Concord that night. In the morning, they planned to surprise the colonists and **seize** the guns.

    (A) fix   (C) take by force

    (B) unload   (D) look up to

5. For a few seconds, no one moved. Then someone fired a shot. This was followed by hundreds of shots. Ten colonists were killed. This is how the colonists began their **rebellion** against England.

    (A) decision about something   (C) long discussion with an enemy

    (B) important meeting with someone   (D) war against your government

6. They met the British troops at Concord's North Bridge. This time the battle ended differently. Many British soldiers were **wounded** or killed and the British army moved back.

    (A) hurt or injured   (C) confused

    (B) lost and afraid   (D) strengthened

Asking Yourself Questions

Asking yourself questions as you read is important. It helps you know what information you should look for and gives you ideas to discuss with other people. Possible question starters are *Who? What? Where? When? How? Why?* For example:

> On the night of April 18, General Gage, the British governor of Massachusetts, heard that colonists were hiding guns in Lexington and Concord, two towns near Boston. He was afraid that they were planning an attack.

How did he find out?

Why did they want to attack?

Was Gage a colonist too? Did he live in England?

1. Read the paragraph below. Ask yourself questions as you read. Draw a line from each box to the sentence you are asking about.

> While the British troops were getting ready, a colonist named Paul Revere got on his horse and rode off. He wanted to warn the men who were guarding the guns in Lexington and Concord. He left four hours before the British troops. Revere arrived in Lexington early in the morning. When 700 British soldiers arrived later, 70 colonists with guns met them.

Question 1

Question 2

Question 3

2. Reread the reading selection on pages 22 and 23. Ask questions as you read about things that confuse you or interest you, or about things you are not sure of. Write these questions on a piece of paper.

3. Work in groups. Ask your group members to help you answer your questions.

Peace and War

Read the definitions below of four words that are related to serious agreements and disagreements between people and nations.

feud /fjud/ *noun* a disagreement or strong dislike between people or groups

The two families are having a feud over building a fence.

hostile /ˈhastəl/ *adjective* angry and very unfriendly

The rioters were very hostile and threw rocks at police.

militia /məˈlɪʃə/ *noun* an army made up of people who are not regular soldiers but fight in an emergency

The general sent for the militia as soon as he heard the gunfire.

treaty /ˈtriti/ *noun* (plural **treaties**) an agreement between two or more countries

The treaty between the United States and Canada ended their disagreement over the border.

Fill in each blank with the correct word from above.

1. War was coming. The colonists had no army so they secretly formed a
_____. This way they were ready to fight.

2. Unfair taxes caused the _____ between England and the 13 American colonies. This disagreement was leading to war.

3. The colonists set British goods on fire, frightened British officials, and did other _____ things.

4. In 1783, England signed a _____ with the American colonies. It gave the colonies their independence and ended the American Revolution.

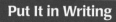

Write a short report. Pretend that you are one of the British soldiers at Lexington and Concord. Tell your governor, General Gage, what happened to you in both locations. Try to use the words *militia* and *hostile* in your paragraph.

Reading Comprehension Tests

Some tests ask you to read a passage and answer questions about it. Try reading the questions first. Then *skim*, or look quickly through the reading, to find the parts that have the answers. You should read these parts more carefully.

Practice this strategy on the sample question. Read the question first. Then read the passage.

Directions: Read the selection below. Choose the best answer to the question.

> British soldiers in Boston did not get paid very much. So they often took jobs to earn extra money. Because they worked for very little money, they took jobs away from Americans. This caused angry arguments on the streets of Boston. People called the British soldiers lobsters because their red coats were the same color as this cooked seafood. The soldiers called the colonists Yankees.

Sample Question

S. The colonists called the British soldiers lobsters because

Ⓐ they often ate lobster for lunch.

Ⓑ lobsters were ugly animals.

Ⓒ most lobsters come from England.

Ⓓ cooked lobsters are the same color as the soldiers' coats.

Did reading the question first help you to answer the question?
The correct answer is on page 119.

Go on

PRACTICE TEST

Directions: Read the selection below. Choose the best answer to each question.

Paul Revere is famous because he warned the colonists that the British troops were coming. However, many people do not know he was also very skillful at making things. In his Boston shop he made beautiful silver bowls, pitchers, and spoons. Rich families paid him well for fancy tea sets with matching trays. For an extra charge, Revere decorated the pieces with the family's initials. He often signed his work by stamping "REVERE" or "PR" somewhere on it. Today a pitcher or spoon made by Paul Revere sells for thousands of dollars.

The large tea sets Revere made for his wealthy customers are the most valuable. But most of his silver pieces were small and not very fancy. He made thousands of buckles, buttons, and tiny tobacco boxes. He even made a child's whistle and a chain for a pet squirrel.

1. A good title for this passage would be

   Ⓐ How to Make Silver Bowls

   Ⓑ The Paul Revere Most People Don't Know

   Ⓒ Workers in Early Boston

   Ⓓ Squirrels Can Make Good Pets

2. Most of Paul Revere's silver pieces were

   Ⓐ given to friends.

   Ⓑ made for rich families.

   Ⓒ sold in England.

   Ⓓ small and simple.

3. How did Revere let people know he made an object?

   Ⓐ He wrote his name on a label and attached it to the object.

   Ⓑ He gave the buyer a letter saying it was his work.

   Ⓒ He put his name or initials on the object.

   Ⓓ He put notices in the newspaper.

4. Revere charged more for a silver bowl if the customer

   Ⓐ wanted his or her initials on it.

   Ⓑ was wealthy.

   Ⓒ was English.

   Ⓓ needed it in a hurry.

Correct answers are on page 119.

STOP

John Hancock signs the Declaration of Independence.

The Declaration of Independence

Reading Skill:
Noticing the Sequence of Events

Expand Your Vocabulary:
The Right to Vote

Get Ready to Read

1. Think about the word *independence*. Write two words or sentences that help explain what it means to you.

   _____

   _____

2. Look at the picture above and the words under it. List two things you think you will learn about the Declaration of Independence in this reading.

   _____

   _____

🎧 The Declaration of Independence

1   On June 7, 1776, a group of men met in Philadelphia, Pennsylvania. They were the **representatives** of the people in the 13 American colonies. They were there to make a decision: Should the colonies separate from England and form a new, independent
5   nation? In other words, should the colonists declare their independence from England?

     General George Washington's American army was already fighting the British. But England had a large, powerful army and navy. Washington's army did not have many supplies. If the colonies
10   lost, England was probably going to kill the men who voted for independence. Therefore, voting for independence was dangerous. Most of the representatives still thought independence was a good idea, but they decided to wait to vote until July 2. In the meantime, the representatives asked Thomas Jefferson to write a Declaration of
15   Independence. That **document** was going to explain the reasons why the colonists wanted to be free from England.

     Jefferson worked for two weeks to write the Declaration of Independence. On July 2, 1776, some men argued for independence. Other men argued against it. After a long **debate**, the
20   representatives voted for independence. Two days later, on July 4, Jefferson's Declaration of Independence was given to John Dunlap, a Philadelphia printer. Dunlap printed about 200 copies. One copy was rushed to General Washington, who read it to his troops on July 9. Other copies were passed around the streets of Philadelphia. The
25   Declaration of Independence powerfully states that people have certain rights that the government cannot take away. It also says that the people, not kings, should make laws. The most unforgettable part, however, are the words "We hold these truths to be self-evident, that all men are created equal." In other words, all
30   people have the same rights. The **principles** in the Declaration completely changed the way government worked. They became the **foundation** of democracy in the United States.

It took seven years for the United States to **defeat** the British and become an independent country in 1783. In many ways, the United States is still trying to become a nation like the one promised in the Declaration of Independence.

Today, there are still 25 original copies of the Declaration of Independence printed by Dunlap. In 1989 someone found the 25th copy behind an old picture. He sold it for more than $8 million to Norman Lear, a television producer. Lear promised to share it with the American people. That copy is now being shown around the country to remind us of our history and our goals as a nation.

The Declaration of Independence

Check Your Understanding

1. How long did Jefferson work on the Declaration of Independence?

_____

2. What was the purpose of the Declaration of Independence?

_____

 3. What do you think the writer meant when he wrote, "In many ways, the United States is still trying to become a nation like the one promised in the Declaration of Independence"?

_____

_____

The Declaration of Independence   31

What is the meaning of each word in blue? Fill in the correct bubble.

1. On June 7, 1776, a group of men met in Philadelphia. They were the **representatives** of the people in the 13 American colonies.

   (A) men who travel a long distance   (C) anyone from another state

   (B) people who are elected to speak for others   (D) people who were loyal to England

2. In the meantime, the representatives asked Thomas Jefferson to write a Declaration of Independence. That **document** was going to explain the reasons why the colonists wanted to be free from England.

   (A) speech   (C) vote

   (B) loud alarm   (D) important paper

3. On July 2, 1776, some men argued for independence. Other men argued against it. After a long **debate**, the representatives voted for independence.

   (A) silence   (C) argument or discussion

   (B) game   (D) pause or break

4. It also says that the people, not kings, should make laws. The most unforgettable part, however, are the words "We hold these truths to be self-evident, that all men are created equal." In other words, all people have the same rights. The **principles** in the Declaration completely changed the way government worked.

   (A) ideas about what is right or wrong   (C) battles for freedom

   (B) laws   (D) orders from kings

5. These principles completely changed the way government worked. They became the **foundation** of democracy in the United States.

   (A) basic belief or fact   (C) written report

   (B) confusing statement   (D) long explanation

6. It took seven years for the United States to **defeat** the British and become an independent country.

   (A) lose to   (C) hide from

   (B) make friends with   (D) win against or beat

Noticing the Sequence of Events

As you read, notice the *sequence of events*, or order in which things happen. Sometimes the writer will tell the date or time of an event. Phrases like *two days later* tell how much time passed before the next event.

A timeline places dates and events in order on a line. Write these events next to the matching date on the timeline below. One has been done for you.

Washington read the Declaration to his army.

The representatives met in Philadelphia.

~~The Declaration of Independence was printed.~~

The colonists defeated the British.

The representatives voted for independence.

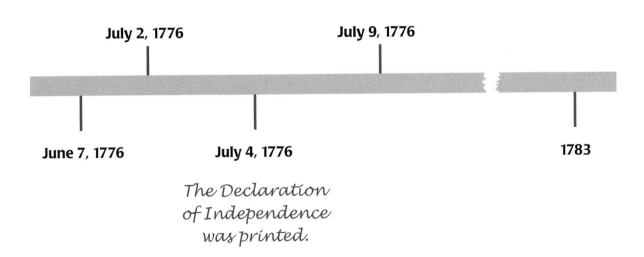

July 2, 1776   July 9, 1776

June 7, 1776   July 4, 1776   1783

The Declaration of Independence was printed.

The Right to Vote

Read the definitions below of four words that are related to voting.

ballot /ˈbælət/ *noun* a piece of paper on which someone marks his or her vote

The ballot listed the names of the three people running for the office.

candidate /ˈkændɪˌdeɪt/ *noun* a person who is trying to be elected to a government job

The candidate for mayor spoke at the meeting.

citizen /ˈsɪtɪzən/ *noun* a legal member of a particular country

A citizen of the United States has the right to vote.

issue /ˈɪʃu/ *noun* a subject that people disagree about

New taxes will be an important issue in the next election.

Write the correct word from above next to each clue.

_____ **1.** This is counted after an election.

_____ **2.** Improving the economy is an example of this.

_____ **3.** This person's name is on a ballot.

_____ **4.** Someone who moves to a new country from another country must pass a test to become this.

Put It in Writing

Write a short speech asking students to vote for you in a school election. Try to use one or more of the words you learned in this chapter.

CHAPTER

6

Benjamin Banneker helped plan the city of Washington, D.C.

Benjamin Banneker: Self-Taught Genius

Reading Skill:
Noticing Cause and Effect

Expand Your Vocabulary:
The Branches of Government

Get Ready to Read

1. What knowledge and skills does a person need to do each of these jobs?

   clock maker _____

   astronomer _____

   weather forecaster _____

   city designer/planner _____

2. Benjamin Banneker is called a self-taught genius. What do you think you will learn about him in this reading?

   _____

Benjamin Banneker: Self-Taught Genius   **35**

🎧 Benjamin Banneker: Self-Taught Genius

1   In 1753 a young African American man received a gift that changed his life. The young man was Benjamin Banneker. The gift was a watch. The tiny wheels in the watch interested him very much, so he took the watch apart. Banneker examined each part of the watch and studied how it worked. When 5 he put the watch back together, it worked perfectly. Then he copied all of the parts in wood and built an **identical** clock. It was the first striking clock made completely in America. This wooden clock worked perfectly for 40 years. Banneker's **career** as an inventor, astronomer, and mathematician was just beginning.

10   Like most African Americans at the time, Banneker had very little education. So he studied books on mathematics and map-making and taught himself. He read books about the stars and how they moved across the sky. He borrowed special **instruments** from a friend to study the moon and stars through a hole he cut in the roof of his house. Soon he began publishing 15 books called almanacs with information about the stars, the weather, and other topics. As a result of these popular books, Banneker became famous throughout the United States and as far away as France and England.

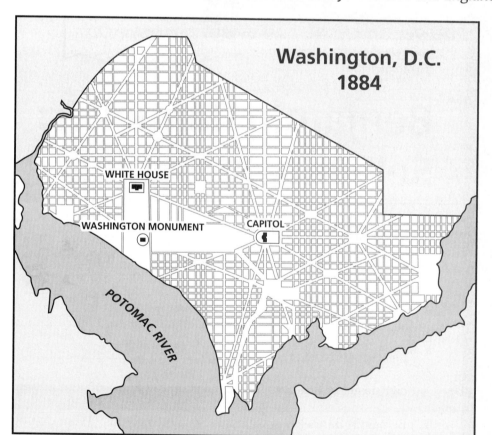

L'Enfant's complex plan for Washington, D.C., which Banneker remembered

In 1790, Philadelphia, Pennsylvania, was the **capital** of the United States. The lawmakers
20 decided to build a new city in the District of Columbia and make it the capital. President George Washington **appointed** Banneker to help a designer plan Washington, D.C. The designer, Pierre L'Enfant, created a very **complex**
25 set of plans for the city. It had many parts that had to be measured exactly. The city was designed in the shape of a diamond. The Washington Monument was at the center of the diamond. Streets spread out from several circles
30 and formed patterns. But before the plans were finished, L'Enfant was fired. He took all the plans when he left. Banneker amazed everyone by remembering all the plans and drawing them again. This saved the U.S. government the time
35 and cost of a new design. But more importantly, Washington, D.C., is the beautiful city it is today because of the work of Banneker.

The Benjamin Banneker stamp

When he died in 1806, Banneker was famous all over the world. In 1980 the United States Postal Service created the Benjamin Banneker stamp to
40 honor him and remind us all of the work he did for the nation's capital.

Check Your Understanding

1. What gift changed Benjamin Banneker's life?

   _____

2. What made Banneker famous in England and France as well as the United States?

   _____

3. Give three reasons that explain why Banneker is called a self-taught genius.

   _____

   _____

   _____

What is the meaning of each word in blue? Fill in the correct bubble.

1. Then he copied all of the parts in wood and built an **identical** clock.

   Ⓐ easy to describe   Ⓒ slow moving

   Ⓑ improved   Ⓓ exactly the same

2. This wooden clock worked perfectly for 40 years. Banneker's **career** as an inventor, astronomer, and mathematician was just beginning.

   Ⓐ education in schools and colleges   Ⓒ teaching activities

   Ⓑ job or profession for a long time   Ⓓ time spent alone

3. He borrowed special **instruments** from a friend to study the moon and stars through a hole he cut in the roof of his house.

   Ⓐ materials used in buildings   Ⓒ tools used for scientific work

   Ⓑ maps   Ⓓ parts of a watch

4. In 1790, Philadelphia, Pennsylvania, was the **capital** of the United States. The lawmakers decided to build a new city and make it the capital.

   Ⓐ unexplored land   Ⓒ area of farms and small homes

   Ⓑ place near a river   Ⓓ city where the government is

5. President George Washington **appointed** Banneker to help a designer plan Washington, D.C.

   Ⓐ picked someone for a job   Ⓒ talked about someone

   Ⓑ sent someone away   Ⓓ forgot someone

6. The designer, Pierre L'Enfant, created a very **complex** set of plans for the city. It had many parts that had to be measured exactly.

   Ⓐ copied from an earlier example   Ⓒ easily changed or replaced

   Ⓑ made up of many small details   Ⓓ beautifully drawn

Noticing Cause and Effect

A *cause* is the reason something happens. An *effect* is the thing that happens.

    Cause: The watch interested Benjamin Banneker.

    Effect: He took it apart and copied it.

Words like *as a result, because, for that reason, so,* and *therefore* signal a cause and an effect.

Read the reading selection again and look for causes and effects. Write the missing causes and effects in the chart below. The first one has been done for you.

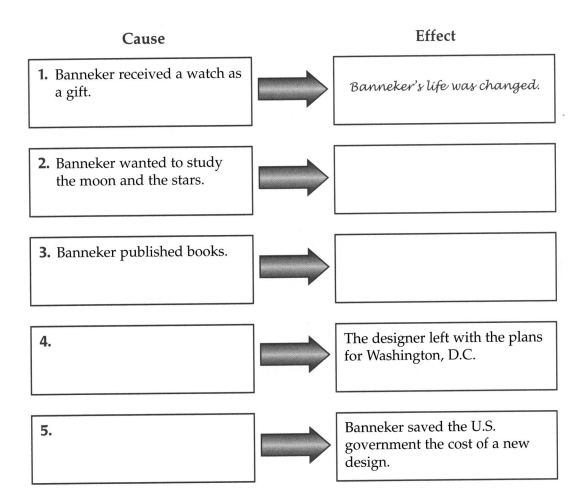

Cause		Effect
1. Banneker received a watch as a gift.	→	*Banneker's life was changed.*
2. Banneker wanted to study the moon and the stars.	→	
3. Banneker published books.	→	
4.	→	The designer left with the plans for Washington, D.C.
5.	→	Banneker saved the U.S. government the cost of a new design.

The Branches of Government

President	Congress	Supreme Court

House of Representatives	Senate

Read the definitions of these parts of our government below.

Congress /ˈkɑngrəs/ *noun* the branch of the U.S. government that votes on laws for the president to approve

House of Representitives /ˌhaʊs əv rɛprɪˈzɛntətɪvz/ *noun* the larger of the two parts of Congress. States with more people have more representatives.

Senate /ˈsɛnət/ *noun* the smaller of the two parts of Congress. Each state elects two senators.

Supreme Court /səˌprim ˈkɔrt/ *noun* the court of law with power and control over all other courts

Write the correct word from above next to each clue.

_____ **1.** Judges are appointed to this part of the government.

_____ **2.** There are two parts, or houses, in this branch of government.

_____ **3.** The number of people a state sends to this depends on the number of people in the state.

_____ **4.** The states of Texas, Nevada, and Kansas each send two people to this.

Write a paragraph about a new law. Pretend you are a member of Congress. Describe a law that you want to pass. Try to use one or more of the words above.

Prefixes and Suffixes

A *prefix* is a word part with meaning that is added to the beginning of a word. The prefix changes the meaning of the word.

Prefix	Meaning	Example	Meaning
in-	not	incorrect	not correct
mis-	wrong	miscount	count wrong
pre-	before	prepay	pay before
re-	again	reuse	use again
un-	not	unequal	not equal

Write the meaning of the underlined word in each of these sentences. Check your answers with a dictionary.

1. The colonists thought the British tax was <u>unfair</u>.

   _____

2. The British <u>misunderstood</u> how strongly the colonists felt.

   _____

3. Jefferson asked Benjamin Franklin to <u>review</u> what he wrote.

   _____

4. Washington <u>previewed</u> the Declaration of Independence before reading it to his troops.

   _____

5. After the Revolutionary War the United States became an <u>independent</u> nation.

   _____

Add a prefix to each word below to make a new word. Write the meaning of the new word. You can check your answers with a dictionary.

	New Word	Meaning
6. kind	_____	_____
7. build	_____	_____
8. read	_____	_____
9. complete	_____	_____

A *suffix* is a word part with meaning that is added to the end of a word. The suffix changes the meaning of the word. It can also change how the word is used in a sentence.

Suffix	Meaning	Example	Meaning
-able	able to be done	breakable	able to be broken
-er, -or	someone who does	inventor	someone who invents
-ful	full of	careful	full of care
-ion	action, process, or result of	education	process of educating
-less	without	worthless	without worth

Write the meaning of the underlined word in each of these sentences. Check your answers with a dictionary.

10. Washington, D.C., is a beautiful city.

_____

11. Our trip to the capital was very enjoyable.

_____

12. The governor spoke to us for ten minutes.

_____

13. Without the parks and monuments, the capital would seem lifeless.

_____

14. We asked for an explanation of how the building was made.

_____

Add a suffix to each word below to make a new word. Write the meaning of the new word. You can check your answers with a dictionary.

	New Word	Meaning
15. connect	_____	_____
16. teach	_____	_____
17. cheer	_____	_____
18. thought	_____	_____

*Sacagawea leads Meriwether Lewis and
William Clark over the mountains.*

Sacagawea and the Path to the Sea

Reading Skill:
Noticing the
Sequence of
Events

**Expand Your
Vocabulary:**
Geography

Get Ready to Read

1. Have you ever needed someone to help you out of a difficult
    situation? What did the person do? Why couldn't you help yourself?

    _____

    _____

2. The explorers in the picture must cross the mountains. List two
    problems they will have to solve. How could someone help them?

    _____

    _____

🎧 Sacagawea and the Path to the Sea

1   In May 1804, a group of 40 **courageous** men left Saint Louis, Missouri, on an amazing and dangerous trip. They were going to travel thousands of miles searching for a path from the Mississippi River, in the middle of the country, to the Pacific Ocean. No one knew then that a 16-year-old girl and

5   her baby were going to help them.

In 1804, people in the United States did not know much about the land and the people west of the Mississippi River. The Europeans who were there before told amazing stories of unusual people, strange animals, and powerful rivers. President Thomas Jefferson asked Meriwether Lewis and William Clark

10 to **assemble** a group of men and find out what was really there.

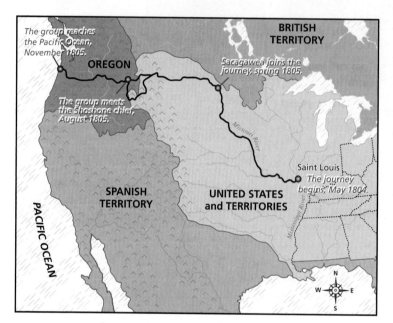

Lewis and Clark's route from Saint Louis, Missouri, to the Pacific Ocean

The trip was difficult from the start. The men worked hard to push the boats against the strong river current. They hunted for food every day. It was not easy to keep their gunpowder and equipment dry. Worst of all, they were afraid that hostile enemies might attack and kill them.

15 In November, the men built a camp near a Native American village. Here they met a French trader, and his wife, Sacagawea /ˌsækədʒəˈwiə/. Sacagawea was born in the Shoshone /ʃoʊˈʃoʊni/ tribe, a group of Native Americans in the Northwest. But an enemy tribe **captured** her when she was 12 years old. She could now speak several Native American languages. So

20 Lewis and Clark invited Sacagawea, her husband, and their new baby son to join them.

In the spring, the group continued the **journey** west. Sacagawea was very helpful. She gathered **nutritious** plants for the men to eat. When a boat sank, Sacagawea was able to save valuable papers and supplies.

25 Most importantly, when groups of Native Americans saw the girl and her baby, they knew the explorers did not want to harm them and let them pass.

By August, the explorers were near the Pacific Ocean, but there were large mountains in front of

30 them. They could not cross this mountain **barrier** without horses, supplies, and guides. But Sacagawea helped them again. She led them to the land of the Shoshone. Her brother was the chief there. He gave Lewis and Clark everything they needed to

35 cross the mountains. Two months later, they reached the Pacific Ocean.

The Sacagawea gold dollar coin

Lewis then asked everyone to vote on where to camp for the winter. He was so grateful for Sacagawea's

40 help that he gave her a full vote. She was the first woman in American history to vote. It took over a hundred years before the 19th Amendment gave all American women the right to vote.

Check Your Understanding

1. How did the Native Americans know that Lewis and Clark's group did not want to harm them?

_____

2. What three things did Sacagawea's brother, the Shoshone chief, give Lewis and Clark that helped them cross the mountains?

_____

3. After the explorers reached the Pacific, why do you think they built a camp for the winter instead of returning home?

_____

What is the meaning of each word in blue? Fill in the correct bubble.

1. In May 1804, a group of 40 **courageous** men left Saint Louis, Missouri, on an amazing and dangerous trip.

   (A) young   (C) brave

   (B) strong   (D) foolish

2. President Thomas Jefferson asked Meriwether Lewis and William Clark to **assemble** a group of men and find out what was really there.

   (A) chase away   (C) frighten

   (B) praise   (D) put together

3. Sacagawea was born in the Shoshone tribe, a group of Native Americans in the Northwest. But an enemy tribe **captured** her when she was 12 years old.

   (A) admired her   (C) set her free

   (B) took her as a prisoner   (D) taught her

4. In the spring, the group continued the **journey** west.

   (A) long trip   (C) ride

   (B) search   (D) battle

5. Sacagawea was very helpful. She gathered **nutritious** plants for the men to eat.

   (A) unusual   (C) healthy

   (B) delicious   (D) tall

6. By August, the explorers were near the Pacific Ocean, but there were large mountains in front of them. They could not cross this mountain **barrier** without horses, supplies, and guides.

   (A) place where supplies   (C) something that blocks
       are kept   your way

   (B) hidden path through   (D) enemy attack
       a mountain

Noticing the Sequence of Events

As you read, notice the *sequence of events,* or order in which things happen. Sometimes the writer will tell the date or time of an event. Words such as *then, next, later,* and *afterwards* can also help you follow the sequence of events. For example:

> *In November,* the men built a camp in a Native American village... *In the spring,* the group continued the journey west.

These events from *Sacagawea and the Path to the Sea* **are not in order. Recopy the sentences in the correct order to form a paragraph. The first one has been done for you.**

- Then the Shoshone chief gave the explorers what they needed to cross the mountains.

- Several months later, Sacagawea joined the group.

- Finally, Lewis and Clark reached the Pacific Ocean.

- ~~The explorers left Saint Louis in May 1804.~~

- Later on, Sacagawea saved valuable papers and supplies when a boat sank.

The explorers left Saint Louis in May 1804.

_____

_____

_____

_____

_____

_____

_____

Geography

Read the definitions below of four kinds of land.

canyon /ˈkænjən/ *noun* a narrow area of low land between steep cliffs

The echo bounced off the walls of the narrow canyon.

desert /ˈdɛzərt/ *noun* a dry area often covered with sand with few plants

The hikers moved slowly through the desert looking for water.

prairie /ˈprɛri/ *noun* a wide area of flat land covered with grass but few trees

The wagons moved quickly over the smooth prairie.

valley /ˈvæli/ *noun* a low area of land between two mountains or hills

The heavy rains caused floods in the valley.

Write the word from the list that describes each picture.

1. _____

3. _____

2. _____

4. _____

Write a paragraph about an area of the world you have visited or want to visit. Try to use one or more of the words above.

Francis Scott Key sees the U.S. flag at Fort McHenry after the British attack on Baltimore Harbor in 1814.

The Star-Spangled Banner: Our National Anthem

Reading Skill:
Making a Personal Connection

Expand Your Vocabulary:
Literature

Get Ready to Read

1. How do you feel when you see the flag of the United States or another country that you know? How do you feel when you hear the national anthem (national song)?

   _____

   _____

2. Look at the picture above and read the title of this chapter. Write two things you expect to learn as you read "The Star-Spangled Banner: Our National Anthem."

   _____

   _____

The Star-Spangled Banner: Our National Anthem

1   It was 1814. All day and all night, the sound of cannons filled the air. Bright explosions lit up the sky. British ships were shooting cannon balls into the fort in the harbor. The British commander was **determined** to capture the city of Baltimore, Maryland. Only Fort McHenry was stopping the British.

5   From a ship far away, a young lawyer from Washington, D.C., named Francis Scott Key watched the battle. He came to the ship earlier to ask the British to **release** a friend who was their prisoner. Now he couldn't go back to land because of this large battle in Baltimore Harbor.

On the morning of September 14, 1814, the shooting

10   stopped. Slowly the smoke began to disappear, and the sun came up. Key stared in the direction of the fort. He didn't think that the Americans inside were still alive. Little by little he could

15   see the damaged walls. Then he saw what he was hoping to see—the flag of the United States of America. The flag was ripped and burned in several places, but it was still there. That

20   meant that the defenders were there too. They did not **surrender** to the British.

A cannon

Key was excited by what he saw. He was an **amateur** poet who liked to write simple poems. But he was now about to write a poem that later made him

25   famous—*The Star-Spangled Banner*. He quickly looked around for something to write on. He found an envelope and began writing,

Oh, say can you see by the dawn's early light
What so proudly we hailed at the twilight's last gleaming?

Key finished the poem after he returned to Baltimore. He printed it and

30   **distributed** it to people in the city with a note saying that the poem should be sung. *The Star-Spangled Banner* quickly became well known and people often sang it at **patriotic** events. During the Civil War, Union soldiers sang it to show

their love for their country.
Around 1903, bands began
35 playing *The Star-Spangled Banner* before baseball games.
In 1931, *The Star-Spangled Banner* became the American national anthem, the official
40 song of the United States.

Colonel Armistead, the commander of Fort McHenry, kept the flag after the battle. He gave it to his grandson,
45 Eben Appleton. In 1907, Appleton gave the flag to the National Museum of American History in Washington, D.C. You can see it hanging in the
50 museum today.

The flag from Fort McHenry

Check Your Understanding

1. Answer these questions about the writing of *The Star-Spangled Banner*. Write your answer in the ovals. One has been done for you.

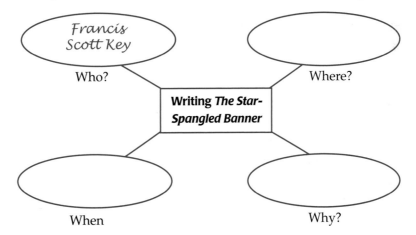

Francis Scott Key

Who?

Where?

Writing *The Star-Spangled Banner*

When

Why?

2. Why was it so important for Key to see the U.S. flag in the morning? What did it mean?

What is the meaning of each word in blue? Fill in the correct bubble.

1. British ships were shooting cannon balls into the fort in the harbor. The British commander was **determined** to capture the city of Baltimore, Maryland. Only Fort McHenry was stopping the British.

   (A) not interested in doing something

   (B) unable to do something

   (C) wanting to do something very much

   (D) able to do something easily

2. He came to the ship earlier to ask the British to **release** a friend who was their prisoner.

   (A) punish him

   (B) let him go

   (C) ask about him

   (D) delay him

3. The defenders were there too. They did not **surrender** to the British.

   (A) fight bravely

   (B) attack

   (C) give up

   (D) answer

4. He was an **amateur** poet who liked to write simple poems. But he was now about to write a poem that later made him famous—*The Star-Spangled Banner.*

   (A) very skillful

   (B) not very skillful

   (C) famous

   (D) foolish

5. Key finished the poem after he returned to Baltimore. He printed it and **distributed** it to people in the city with a note saying that the poem should be sung.

   (A) divided it into parts

   (B) kept it in a secret place

   (C) gave it to a lot of people

   (D) read it aloud to friends

6. *The Star-Spangled Banner* quickly became well known and people often sang it at **patriotic** events. During the Civil War, Union soldiers sang it to show their love for their country.

   (A) showing love for your country

   (B) connected to sports

   (C) happening during a war

   (D) sad

Making a Personal Connection

It is important to look for ways to connect what you read with your own life. This makes reading more interesting and helps you remember more. Example:

> It was 1814. All day and all night, the sound of cannons filled the air. Bright explosions lit up the sky. British ships were shooting cannon balls into the fort in the harbor.

This reminds me of the fireworks I saw last year.

1. Read the following paragraph. Think of two ways these events connect to your life. Write the connections between the lines. You might begin with "This reminds me of . . . ." or "This is just like . . . ."

On the morning of September 14, 1814, the shooting stopped. Slowly the smoke began to disappear, and the sun came up. Key stared in the direction of the fort. He didn't think that the Americans inside were still alive. Little by little he could see the damaged walls. Then he saw what he was hoping to see—the flag of the United States of America. The flag was ripped and burned in several places, but it was still there. That meant that the defenders were there too. They did not surrender to the British.

2. Reread the reading selection on pages 50 and 51. Write any other connections to your life that you find. Share them with a partner.

_____

_____

Literature

Read the definitions below of four kinds of literature.

autobiography /ˌɔtoʊbaɪˈɑgrəfi/ *noun* (plural **autobiographies**) the story of someone's life written by that person

The teacher read parts of Benjamin Franklin's autobiography to us.

biography /baɪˈɑgrəfi/ *noun* (plural **biographies**) the story of someone's life written by another person

David Adler's biography of Lou Gehrig is called Lou Gehrig: The Luckiest Man.

fiction /ˈfɪkʃən/ *noun* books or stories that are invented or made up

The library keeps fiction on separate shelves.

nonfiction /nɑnˈfɪkʃən/ *noun* books or articles about facts or real events

An author must gather facts before writing nonfiction.

Write the word from above that describes each book.

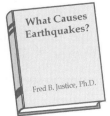

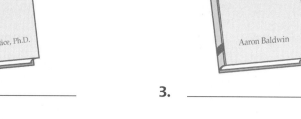

1. _____

3. _____

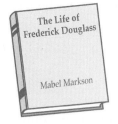

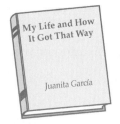

2. _____

4. _____

Write a paragraph that could be part of your autobiography. Tell about something interesting that happened in your life.

Vocabulary Tests

Some tests ask you to choose a word that has the SAME meaning as a word in a sentence. Other tests ask you to choose a word that has the OPPOSITE meaning. Always read the directions and examples carefully and remember what the directions ask you to do.

Practice this strategy on these sample questions.

Directions: Choose the word or words that have the same or nearly the same meaning as the underlined word.

Sample Questions

S1. David gave his best friend an expensive gift.

    Ⓐ high-priced

    Ⓑ old

    Ⓒ cheap

    Ⓓ large

S2. Business is good, so the owner wants to expand the store.

    Ⓐ improve

    Ⓑ buy

    Ⓒ make smaller

    Ⓓ make bigger

Directions: Choose the word or words that have the opposite meaning of the underlined word.

Sample Question

S3. If we try hard, we can complete the work this week.

    Ⓐ start

    Ⓑ move away from

    Ⓒ finish

    Ⓓ avoid

S4. A genuine diamond is worth a lot of money.

    Ⓐ beautiful

    Ⓑ unusual

    Ⓒ real

    Ⓓ fake

Did you always remember what the directions asked you to do? The correct answers are on page 119.

Go on

 # PRACTICE TEST

Directions: Choose the word or words that have the opposite meaning of the underlined word.

1. Wrap the <u>fragile</u> glass in thick cloth.
   - Ⓐ strong
   - Ⓑ clear
   - Ⓒ valuable
   - Ⓓ easily broken

2. Fresh fruit is <u>scarce</u> during the cold winter months.
   - Ⓐ expensive
   - Ⓑ seen everywhere
   - Ⓒ beautiful
   - Ⓓ hard to find

3. We <u>seldom</u> watch TV. We usually read instead.
   - Ⓐ never
   - Ⓑ often
   - Ⓒ hardly ever
   - Ⓓ always

4. The little children played in the <u>shallow</u> end of the pool.
   - Ⓐ near
   - Ⓑ not deep
   - Ⓒ wide
   - Ⓓ deep

Directions: Choose the word or words that have the same or nearly the same meaning as the underlined word.

5. The answer to the question was so <u>obvious</u> that everyone got it right.
   - Ⓐ easy to see
   - Ⓑ difficult
   - Ⓒ not important
   - Ⓓ hidden

6. They were <u>exhausted</u> after they hiked up the mountain..
   - Ⓐ rested
   - Ⓑ tired
   - Ⓒ strong
   - Ⓓ surprised

7. I <u>regret</u> not studying harder and failing the test.
   - Ⓐ enjoy
   - Ⓑ believe in
   - Ⓒ feel sorry about
   - Ⓓ suggest

8. The angry strikers will <u>defy</u> any law that forces them back to work.
   - Ⓐ not obey
   - Ⓑ accept
   - Ⓒ explain
   - Ⓓ help

Correct answers are on page 119.

The much larger Mexican army defeats the defenders of the Alamo in Texas.

Remembering the Alamo

Get Ready to Read

1. Have you ever been in a competition that you knew you could not win? What happened?

   _____

   _____

2. Many Americans say, "Remember the Alamo." This is a battle Americans lost. Why do people want to remember a battle that they lost?

   _____

   _____

🎧 Remembering the Alamo

1   Sixty years after the 13 original American colonies declared independence, another declaration of independence was made in Texas. In 1836, the settlers in Texas declared their independence from Mexico.

5   About 1820, people from the United States began moving to the Mexican territory of Tejas /ˈteɪhɑs/. By 1830, there were many more Americans in the territory than Mexicans. The Americans felt no **loyalty** to Mexico. They were used to governing themselves, and unlike the Mexicans, they did not speak Spanish or belong to the Catholic Church. These differences led to many **disputes** with the Mexican government. Mexico was afraid it might lose Tejas, 10   or Texas, as the Americans called it.

At this time, General Antonio López de Santa Anna ruled Mexico. To show his **authority** over Texas, Santa Anna led a large army into Texas. The Alamo, an old mission used as a fort, blocked the road into Texas. About 150 ordinary Texans met to defend the Alamo against Santa Anna's powerful army.

15   Santa Anna sent a message to William Travis, commander of the Alamo's defenders, and told him to surrender. Travis answered by firing a cannon ball. On February 23, 1836, Santa Anna surrounded the Alamo with 1,800 of his troops and began firing cannon balls into the walls. This continued for 12 days. On March 6, Santa Anna began

20   a final **assault**. The defenders quickly stopped shooting. They had no more bullets. But they fought with knives

25   and fists even though they knew they could not win. In the end, nearly all the defenders were killed in the battle.

30   The few Texan **survivors** were captured, and then they were killed too. About 600 of Santa Anna's soldiers were

35   killed or wounded in the attack.

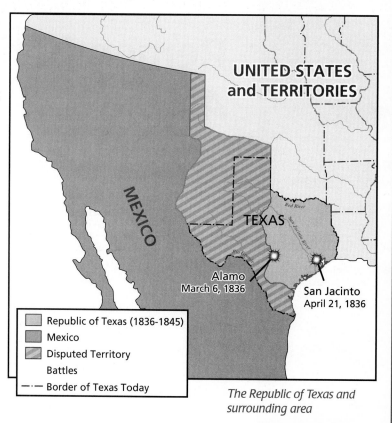

The Republic of Texas and surrounding area

At the same time, in another part of Texas, Sam Houston and other Texas leaders voted to declare Texas independent from Mexico. Six weeks later, Houston learned that Santa

40 Anna's army was camped near the San Jacinto River. Texans wanted **revenge** for the deaths of the Alamo's defenders. Yelling "Remember the Alamo," Houston and 800 men attacked the surprised Mexican army. In just 18 minutes, they killed 630 Mexican soldiers and captured 700 more. Santa Anna himself

45 was captured the next day. Texas was now an independent country.

The Texas flag

The Texas flag had one white star. So the Texans called their new nation the Lone Star Republic. In 1845, this Lone Star Republic joined the

50 United States and became the state of Texas. Today, Texas is called the Lone Star State because of the

55 flag Houston's troops carried into the battle against Mexico.

Actors at the Alamo today dress up as the men who once fought there.

Check Your Understanding

1. Who was the leader of Mexico in 1836?

_____

2. When the Mexicans told the defenders of the Alamo to surrender, what did they do?

_____

 3. Why do you think the Texans yelled, "Remember the Alamo," when they attacked the Mexican army?

_____

_____

What is the meaning of each word in blue? Fill in the correct bubble.

1. The Americans felt no **loyalty** to Mexico. They were used to governing themselves, and unlike the Mexicans, they did not speak Spanish or belong to the Catholic Church.

   Ⓐ desire to visit

   Ⓑ hatred

   Ⓒ love and support

   Ⓓ need to help

2. They were used to governing themselves, and unlike the Mexicans, they did not speak Spanish or belong to the Catholic Church. These differences led to many **disputes** with the Mexican government.

   Ⓐ agreements

   Ⓑ arguments

   Ⓒ acts of friendship

   Ⓓ meetings

3. At this time, General Antonio López de Santa Anna ruled Mexico. To show his **authority** over Texas, Santa Anna led a large army into Texas.

   Ⓐ desire for peace

   Ⓑ ability to write

   Ⓒ strong army

   Ⓓ power and control

4. On February 23, 1836, Santa Anna surrounded the Alamo with 1,800 troops and began firing cannon balls into the walls. This continued for 12 days. On March 6, Santa Anna began a final **assault**.

   Ⓐ loud explosion

   Ⓑ call for help

   Ⓒ discussion

   Ⓓ attack

5. In the end, nearly all the defenders were killed in the battle. The few Texan **survivors** were captured, and then they were killed too.

   Ⓐ people still alive

   Ⓑ dead soldiers

   Ⓒ people in Texas

   Ⓓ government officials

6. Texans wanted **revenge** for the deaths of the Alamo's defenders. Yelling "Remember the Alamo," Houston and 800 men attacked the surprised Mexican army. In just 18 minutes, they killed 630 Mexican soldiers and captured 700 more.

   Ⓐ a peace treaty

   Ⓑ action to punish someone for hurting you

   Ⓒ guns and bullets

   Ⓓ a quiet place to rest

Noticing Details

When you read, pay attention to *details*, the small pieces of information in a paragraph. The details often help you understand the big ideas better.

Work with a partner.

Student A: Read the second paragraph in the reading aloud.

Student B: Listen for the details and write the answers to questions 1 and 2.

Questions	Answers
1. When did Americans start moving into Tejas?	
2. What three things led to problems between the Americans and the Mexican government?	a. b. c.

Change jobs.

Student B: Read the fourth paragraph aloud.

Student A: Listen for the details and write the answers to questions 3 and 4.

Questions	Answers
3. What message did Santa Anna send to the captain of the Alamo?	
4. How long did Santa Anna fire his cannons at the Alamo before the final attack?	

Government

Read the definitions below of four kinds of government.

anarchy /ˈænərki/ *noun* a situation in which there is no government or authority

The earthquake caused a state of anarchy in the country.

democracy /dɪˈmakrəsi/ *noun* a system in which the people can vote to choose the people in their government

Our democracy was established by the Constitution.

dictatorship /dɪkˈteɪtərˌʃɪp/ *noun* government by one person with complete power

The army's action ended the cruel dictatorship.

monarchy /ˈmanərki/ *noun* government by a king or queen

The English monarchy has lasted nearly a thousand years.

Read each headline below. What type of government does it describe? Write the correct word from above.

Government officials leave the country
Rioters burn and steal

Voters to choose members of Congress today

1. _____   3. _____

King Charles II crowned in a ceremony today

General Maxum orders schools and businesses to close and people to stay off the street

2. _____   4. _____

Write a paragraph about the type of government you think is best. Give reasons for your choice.

Cherokees travel to Indian Territory along the Trail of Tears.

The Trail of Tears

Reading Skill:
Finding the Main Idea

Expand You Vocabulary:
Courts of Law

Get Ready to Read

1. Why do people sometimes have to leave their homes and live in a place they don't like?

    _____

    _____

2. Look at the picture and read the title of this chapter. Write two questions you think the reading will answer about the people in the picture.

    _____

    _____

🎧 The Trail of Tears

1   In 1830, the U.S. Congress was considering a new law called the Indian Removal Act. It was going to force Native Americans to give up their land and move west. Some Congressmen **opposed** the law and spoke out angrily against it, but it passed anyway. President Andrew Jackson quickly signed it.

5   Because of this new law, Native Americans in the Southeast were moved to a dry, empty land. This "Indian Territory" covered what is now Oklahoma and parts of Kansas and Nebraska. However, when the state of Georgia tried to move the Cherokee tribe, they **refused** to go. They felt the law was wrong and decided to **challenge** it in the U.S. Supreme Court. In 1832, the court

10   ruled that Georgia could not legally move the Cherokees and take their land. President Jackson was very angry. He decided to ignore the court's decision.

Jackson found a small group of Cherokees who were willing to sign a treaty and move west. They did not represent the large **majority** of Cherokees who refused to move. The U.S. Senate had to approve Jackson's

15   treaty before it could become law. By now, many people felt that the treatment of Native Americans was wrong. Even so, the Senate **ratified** the treaty—by just one vote. That was all Jackson needed.

In 1838, the U.S. army began breaking into Cherokees' homes. Soldiers took men, women, and children to prison camps. Sometimes they had only the

20   clothes they were wearing. As the Cherokees were led away, thieves stole their

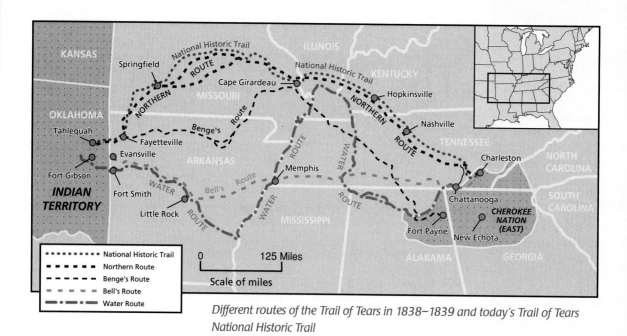

Different routes of the Trail of Tears in 1838–1839 and today's Trail of Tears National Historic Trail

belongings and burned their homes. In the end, the camps held 16,000 Cherokees. On a cold, rainy morning in October, they were loaded into 645 wagons. Then they began a journey of more than a thousand miles.

The Cherokee rose

The winter of 1838–39 was especially cold. For months, soldiers forced the Cherokees to walk through snow and over frozen land. There was little food. Old people became weak. Many people became sick. One of every four Cherokees died on the journey. Many of them were children. The Cherokees called the journey *Nunna daul Tsuny*, "the trail where they cried."

In 1987, the United States made the Trail of Tears a National Historic Trail to remember the Cherokees' hard journey. According to a **legend**, the Cherokee mothers cried many tears for their children along the way. Wherever a tear fell, a white rose grew. Today, white roses, called Cherokee roses, grow along the Trail of Tears. The Cherokee rose is now the official flower of the state of Georgia.

Check Your Understanding

1. What did the Cherokees do when the state of Georgia tried to move them?

   _____

2. At what time of the year were the Cherokees forced to walk to their new homes?

   _____

 3. Why do you think the state of Georgia chose the Cherokee rose as its state flower?

   _____

What is the meaning of each word in blue? Fill in the correct bubble.

1. Some Congressmen **opposed** the law and spoke out angrily against it, but it passed anyway.

   - (A) liked
   - (B) changed
   - (C) did not agree with
   - (D) forgot

2. Because of this new law, Native Americans in the Southeast were moved to a dry, empty land. This "Indian Territory" covered what is now Oklahoma and parts of Kansas and Nebraska. However, when the state of Georgia tried to move the Cherokee tribe, they **refused** to go.

   - (A) said no
   - (B) gave up
   - (C) said yes
   - (D) became friendly

3. They felt the law was wrong and decided to **challenge** it in the U.S. Supreme Court.

   - (A) explain a law
   - (B) avoid obeying a law
   - (C) obey a law
   - (D) ask if a law is legal

4. Jackson found a small group of Cherokees who were willing to sign a treaty and move west. They did not represent the large **majority** of Cherokees who refused to move.

   - (A) more than half
   - (B) military officers
   - (C) male members
   - (D) villages

5. The U.S. Senate had to approve Jackson's treaty before it could become law. By now, many people felt that the treatment of Native Americans was wrong. Even so, the Senate **ratified** the treaty—by just one vote.

   - (A) discussed it
   - (B) delivered it
   - (C) defeated it
   - (D) made it official

6. According to a **legend**, the Cherokee mothers cried many tears for their children along the way. Wherever a tear fell, a white rose grew.

   - (A) story told for many years
   - (B) type of trail
   - (C) unfair law
   - (D) land given to the Native Americans

Finding the Main Idea

A paragraph is a group of sentences about one thing. This one thing is called the topic of the paragraph. The most important thing that the sentences say about that topic is the *main idea*. For example, if the topic of a paragraph is your part-time job, the main idea might be "My part-time job is hard work."

Read these paragraphs from the reading selection. Then answer the question that follows each paragraph.

> The winter of 1838–39 was especially cold. For months, soldiers forced the Cherokees to walk through snow and over frozen land. There was little food. Old people became weak. Many people became sick. One of every four Cherokees died on the journey. Many of them were children. The Cherokees called the journey *Nunna daul Tsuny,* "the trail where they cried."

1. Fill in the bubble of the sentence that states the main idea of the paragraph.

   Ⓐ The Cherokees were not used to bad weather.

   Ⓑ Winter is not a good time to travel.

   Ⓒ Some trails have names.

   Ⓓ The journey was difficult and the Cherokees were treated badly.

> In 1987, the United States made the Trail of Tears a National Historic Trail to remember the Cherokees' hard journey. According to a legend, the Cherokee mothers cried many tears for their children along the way. Wherever a tear fell, a white rose grew. Today, white roses, called Cherokee roses, grow along the Trail of Tears. The Cherokee rose is now the official flower of the state of Georgia.

2. Fill in the bubble of the sentence that states the main idea of the paragraph.

   Ⓐ People today understand how unfairly the Cherokees were treated.

   Ⓑ Cherokee roses are pretty flowers.

   Ⓒ The United States needs more National Historic Trails.

   Ⓓ The Cherokee mothers tried to take good care of their children.

Courts of Law

Read the definitions below of four words that are related to our courts of law.

accuse /əˈkjuz/ *verb* to say that you think someone has broken the law or done something wrong

The store owner accused the men of stealing the money.

defendant /dɪˈfɛndənt/ *noun* a person who is being judged in a court of law

The defendant claimed he did not commit any crime.

jury /ˈdʒɜri/ *noun* (plural **juries**) a group of citizens who are chosen to watch a trial and decide if someone is guilty or not guilty

The jury took four hours to make a decision in the case.

trial /ˈtraɪəl/ *noun* a legal process in which a court of law decides if someone is guilty or not guilty

*The trial is expected to last several weeks. | The man is **on trial** (=being judged in a trial) for murder.*

True or False? Use the definitions. Fill in the correct bubble.

	True	False
1. It is good if someone accuses you of a crime.	T	F
2. A trial takes about five minutes.	T	F
3. A jury is made up of several people.	T	F
4. A defendant is always a person who is guilty of a crime.	T	F

Write a paragraph about a trial or a court show that you saw on television. Try to use one or more of the words above.

Homophones

Words that sound alike but have different meanings and spellings are called *homophones*. These two words are homophones:

sea   a large area of salty water
see   to notice things with your eyes

Read the word and its meaning in the first column. Then write the letter for its homophone in the second column. Check a dictionary to see if the pronunciations are the same. The first one has been done for you.

_c_	1. week	seven days	a. petal	one of the colored parts of a flower
____	2. break	to separate into parts	b. hall	a long area that connects rooms in a building
____	3. scent	a smell or odor	c. weak	not strong
____	4. haul	to carry or pull something heavy	d. one	the number 1
____	5. there	in or to that place	e. wait	to stay in a place until something happens
____	6. weight	how heavy something is	f. hear	to notice sounds with your ears
____	7. piece	a part of something	g. cent	the amount of money a penny is worth
____	8. won	was the best in a game or contest (the past form of *win*)	h. their	belonging to them
____	9. pedal	the part of a bicycle or car that you push with your foot	i. brake	the part of a bicycle or car that makes it stop
____	10. here	in or to this place	j. peace	a time when there is no war or when things are calm

Choose the word in ( ) that fits the meaning of each sentence. Write the word on the line.

1. I will meet you _____ (hear / here) at noon so don't be late.

2. My family has two cats and _____ (one / won) dog.

3. After the rain, the _____ (pedals / petals) of the rose began to open.

4. Her illness made her feel _____ (weak / week) and a little dizzy.

5. The _____ (cent / scent) of pine trees filled the forest air.

6. Try not to _____ (brake / break) the dishes when you wash them.

7. You can sit _____ (their / there) next to Anna.

8. The _____ (peace / piece) ended when the enemy began its attack.

9. The bathroom is down the _____ (haul / hall) on the right.

10. We will _____ (wait / weight) for you at the bus stop.

11. How many _____ (cents / scents) are in a dollar?

12. The Johnsons sold _____ (their /there) house last week.

13. I'll fix the _____ (pedal / petal) on your bike this afternoon.

14. Let me cut a big _____ (peace / piece) of cake for you.

15. Who _____ (one / won) the essay contest?

16. At night, I can _____ (hear / here) the sound of the train.

17. The mechanic checked the _____ (brakes / breaks) on the car.

18. The _____ (wait / weight) of the snow broke a big branch off the tree.

19. They brought a truck to _____ (haul / hall) the dead tree away.

20. The package will arrive next _____ (weak / week).

A mentally ill woman is kept in a prison cell in the 1800s.

Dorothea Dix: Defender of Mentally Ill People

Reading Skill:
Finding Main
Ideas and
Supporting Details

**Expand Your
Vocabulary:**
Health

Get Ready to Read

1. What does it mean to be mentally ill? How are mentally ill people treated today?

   _____

   _____

   _____

2. How do you think mentally ill people were treated differently in the past?

   _____

   _____

   _____

Dorothea Dix: Defender of Mentally Ill People

1   On March 28, 1841, Dorothea Dix entered a jail in East Cambridge, Massachusetts, to teach a religion class. While she was there, she saw things that changed her life and **eventually** changed the lives of thousands of people.

5   The conditions in the jail were awful. Mentally ill people were put in prison cells with violent criminals. There was no heat or fresh air. Cells were dirty and smelled terrible. All of the prisoners, but especially the mentally ill prisoners, were treated cruelly. Some were beaten. When Dix asked the jailer why he allowed these things, he replied that mentally ill people do not feel heat or cold.

10   Dix was very upset by what she saw. She immediately began a **campaign** to change the way mentally ill people were treated. She was sure that many mentally ill people could be cured with proper care. This meant taking them out of jails and putting them in special hospitals. Today that does not seem surprising. But

15   it was a **radical** idea in 1841.

Dix began collecting facts to show to people in the Massachusetts government. She spent nearly two years

20   visiting jails that held mentally ill people all over Massachusetts. She always took clear, **precise** notes on what

25   she saw. In one town, a mentally ill woman was kept in a small cage. In another town, one

30   mentally ill prisoner was chained, while another was kept in a small room for 17 years. In a third town, two mentally ill women lay on

35   straw in wooden beds.

Dorothea Dix

40   In January 1843, Dix gave her report to the state **legislature**. She included examples showing that kindness and proper care could cure mental illness. Her report made the people in the Massachusetts government act. They voted to build and **expand** state hospitals for mentally ill people.

     Dix did not stop there. She quickly started working to change the treatment
45 of mentally ill people in other states. She again visited jails and reported the terrible things she saw. When she began, there were only 13 mental hospitals in the United States. By 1880, there were 123. Dix also helped build 15 schools for mentally ill people, a school for blind people, several nursing schools, and a prison library.

50   Dix continued her work quietly for nearly 40 years. She did not like to be praised and refused to allow a hospital to be named after her. However, a hospital in Raleigh, North Carolina, is named Dix Hill, after Dorothea's grandfather, Dr. Elijah Dix. Today a picture of Dorothea Dix hangs in the hospital.

Check Your Understanding

1. In which state did Dorothea Dix begin her work to help mentally ill people?

   _____

2. What did Dorothea Dix think was necessary to cure mental illness?

   _____

3. Dorothea Dix did not allow any hospitals to be named after her. What does this show about Dorothea Dix?

   _____

   _____

What is the meaning of each word in blue? Fill in the correct bubble.

1. On March 28, 1841, Dorothea Dix entered a jail in East Cambridge, Massachusetts, to teach a religion class. While she was there, she saw things that changed her life and **eventually** changed the lives of thousands of people.

   Ⓐ quietly   Ⓒ possibly

   Ⓑ without any help   Ⓓ in the end

2. Dix was very upset by what she saw. She immediately began a **campaign** to change the way mentally ill people were treated.

   Ⓐ set of actions   Ⓒ long trip

   Ⓑ group of workers   Ⓓ place where people live in tents

3. She was sure that many mentally ill people could be cured with proper care. This meant taking them out of jails and putting them in special hospitals. Today that does not seem surprising. But it was a **radical** idea in 1841.

   Ⓐ completely new and different   Ⓒ very popular

   Ⓑ foolish   Ⓓ simple

4. She always took clear, **precise** notes on what she saw. In one town, a mentally ill woman was kept in a small cage. In another town, one mentally ill prisoner was chained, while another was kept in a small room.

   Ⓐ secret   Ⓒ confusing

   Ⓑ very few   Ⓓ exact and correct

5. In January 1843, Dix gave her report to the state **legislature**. She included examples showing that kindness and proper care could cure mental illness. Her report made the people in the Massachusetts government act.

   Ⓐ a group of doctors   Ⓒ hospital workers

   Ⓑ people who are elected to make laws   Ⓓ voters

6. Her report made the people in the Massachusetts government act. They voted to build and **expand** state hospitals for mentally ill people.

   Ⓐ remove them   Ⓒ explore them

   Ⓑ make them larger   Ⓓ close them

Finding Main Ideas and Supporting Details

The *main idea* of a paragraph is the most important idea. The *supporting details* give information that helps you understand the main idea.

1. The main idea of this paragraph from the reading selection has been underlined. Work with your partner and list three supporting details.

> The conditions in the jail were awful. Mentally ill people were put in prison cells with violent criminals. There was no heat or fresh air. Cells were dirty and smelled terrible. All of the prisoners, but especially the mentally ill prisoners, were treated cruelly. Some were beaten. When Dix asked the jailer why he allowed these things, he replied that mentally ill people do not feel heat or cold.

Main Idea: *The conditions in the jail were awful.*

Supporting Detail: _____

Supporting Detail: _____

Supporting Detail: _____

2. Read this paragraph from the reading selection again. Write the sentence that states the main idea of the paragraph. Then write three supporting details for the main idea.

> Dix began collecting facts to show to people in the Massachusetts government. She spent nearly two years visiting jails that held mentally ill people all over Massachusetts. She always took clear, precise notes on what she saw. In one town, a mentally ill woman was kept in a small cage. In another town, one mentally ill prisoner was chained, while another was kept in a small room for 17 years. In a third town, two mentally ill women lay on straw in wooden beds.

Main Idea: _____

Supporting Detail: _____

Supporting Detail: _____

Supporting Detail: _____

Health

Read the definitions below of four words that are related to health.

> **fever** /ˈfivər/ *noun* a higher than normal body temperature when you are sick
>
> *Putting the ice bag on my head seemed to bring down my fever.*
>
> **infection** /ɪnˈfɛkʃən/ *noun* an illness caused by bacteria or a virus that attacks your body
>
> *Her ear infection caused her to stay home from school.*
>
> **therapy** /ˈθɛrəpi/ *noun* (plural **therapies**) an activity used to heal an injury or cure an illness
>
> *Keeping warm and drinking fresh fruit juices is sometimes the best therapy for a cold.*
>
> **vaccinate** /ˈvæksɪˌneɪt/ *verb* to put a substance into someone's body in order to protect the person from getting a disease
>
> *The doctor will vaccinate the children so they won't get measles.*

Fill in each blank with the correct word from above.

Last week, I asked my doctor to **(1)** _____ me

to keep me from getting the flu. A few days later I began to feel warm. I took my

temperature and found out that I had a(n) **(2)** _____.

The doctor was sure it was not the flu. She thought that I must have gotten a(n)

(3) _____. She was right. A small cut on my hand was

red and sore. The doctor was sure that medicine and rest could cure the problem. She

said that was the only **(4)** _____ that I needed.

Write a paragraph about some things people can do to stay healthy. Try to use one or more of the words above.

A man searches for gold in a river near Sacramento, California.

Gold Fever Hits California

Reading Skill:
Making Inferences

Expand Your Vocabulary:
Geography

Get Ready to Read

1. Imagine that all the men in your town or community suddenly leave. How will the place be different? Write three things that will change.

   _____

   _____

2. What do you hope to learn about the Gold Rush in the reading selection on pages 78 and 79?

   _____

   _____

🎧 Gold Fever Hits California

1 John Sutter saw a chance to make money in 1847. The settlements on the California coast needed **lumber**. Sutter decided to build a mill in the mountains near Sacramento. There he could cut trees into lumber. He could then sell the wood for a nice profit. Sutter sent his partner, James Marshall,
5 to find the best place for the mill. After Marshall found the right place, he hired workers and started to build the mill.

On a rainy January day in 1848, Marshall came to Sutter's office to show him something. He took a cloth out of his pocket and carefully unfolded it. There were several pieces of shiny yellow metal inside. This was
10 gold that Marshall found in the stream below the unfinished mill.

Before Marshall and Sutter could get to the mill, workers found more gold. Sutter asked the workers to keep the gold a secret for six weeks so he could finish building his mill. But a secret like that could not stay hidden for long.

15 When workers began buying shovels and paying for them with gold, people became **suspicious** and started asking questions. The following month,
20 a newspaper reported the discovery of gold at Sutter's mill. Most people **doubted** the story. But soon more men came from the mill with gold in their pockets. People became more

A shovel, pick, and pan that were used by the forty-niners

and more excited. Soon everyone caught gold fever. Workers quit their jobs
25 and left for the gold fields. Businesses throughout California closed. Newspapers stopped being published because the printers joined the search for gold. For months no ships could **depart** from San Francisco. The men who worked on them were off in the mountains looking for gold. Everyone needed tools. Shovels that used to cost one dollar now cost $20. The gold
30 rush was happening!

By September, people in New York and beyond knew about the gold. In 1849, more than 77,000 people rushed to California. These people were called forty-niners. They arrived from the East Coast of the United States, China, South America, and Canada. They all hoped to become rich
35 overnight. Very few people did. The gold that could be taken easily from

streams and fields was soon gone. The gold that was left required hard work for less money. Even so, the forty-
40 niners had a big **influence** on California. The growth in **population** helped California become a state the next year.

Today, California is the
45 home of a mix of people from all around the world. And all around the world today, people still wear blue jeans, the pants that Levi
50 Strauss created for the California miners.

The area of the California Gold Rush

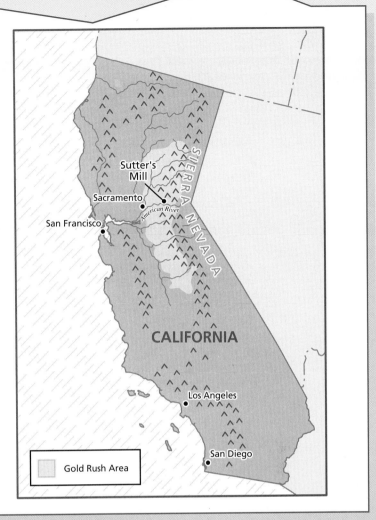

CALIFORNIA

Sutter's Mill

Sacramento

San Francisco

American River

SIERRA NEVADA

Los Angeles

San Diego

Gold Rush Area

Check Your Understanding

1. How did Sutter plan to make money in California?

_____

2. Why did Sutter want his workers to keep the gold a secret?

_____

 3. Why were people paying $20 for a shovel that was only worth a dollar?

_____

What is the meaning of each word in blue? Fill in the correct bubble.

1. John Sutter saw a chance to make money in 1847. The settlements on the California coast needed **lumber**. Sutter decided to build a mill in the mountains near Sacramento. There he could cut trees into lumber.

   Ⓐ farmland   Ⓒ wood used for building

   Ⓑ roads and bridges   Ⓓ books

2. When workers began buying shovels and paying for them with gold, people became **suspicious** and started asking questions.

   Ⓐ tired of hearing so many stories   Ⓒ interested in making money

   Ⓑ believing that something unusual might be true   Ⓓ unable to stop laughing

3. The following month, a newspaper reported the discovery of gold at Sutter's mill. Most people **doubted** the story. But soon more men came from the mill with gold in their pockets.

   Ⓐ told it to other people   Ⓒ didn't think it was true

   Ⓑ believed it immediately   Ⓓ changed it

4. For months no ships could **depart** from San Francisco. The men who worked on them were off in the mountains looking for gold.

   Ⓐ leave   Ⓒ deliver

   Ⓑ arrive   Ⓓ stop

5. Even so, the forty-niners had a big **influence** on California. The growth in population helped California become a state the next year. Today, California is the home of a mix of people from all around the world.

   Ⓐ unknown outcomes   Ⓒ ability to change things

   Ⓑ reason for avoiding something   Ⓓ harmful result

6. The growth in **population** helped California become a state the next year. Today, California is the home of a mix of people from all around the world.

   Ⓐ the number of people living in a place   Ⓒ the amount of taxes people pay

   Ⓑ the area of land   Ⓓ buildings and homes

Making Inferences

You can sometimes use facts that are stated directly in a reading to guess certain facts that are not stated. This is called *making inferences.* Making inferences helps you understand more of what you read.

Stated Fact: The settlements on the California coast needed lumber.
Inference: The people there were building wooden buildings.

Match the stated fact with an inference that could be made from that fact. Write the letter of the inference next to the fact. The first one has been done for you.

Fact	Inference
d **1.** Sutter decided to build a mill in the mountains near Sacramento. There he could cut trees into lumber.	**a.** People did not usually pay for things with gold.
____ **2.** When workers began buying shovels and paying for them with gold, people became suspicious and started asking questions.	**b.** It is easier for a territory to become a state if it has a large population.
____ **3.** But soon more men came to town with gold in their pockets. People became more and more excited.	**c.** People were starting to believe that there really was gold in the mountains.
____ **4.** Shovels that used to cost one dollar now cost $20.	**d.** There are many trees in the mountains near Sacramento.
____ **5.** The growth in population helped California become a state the next year.	**e.** Shovels were needed to search for gold.

Geography

Read the definitions below of four words that are related to geography.

continent /ˈkɑntɪnənt/ *noun* one of the seven large land areas of the Earth; these are Africa, Antarctica, Asia, Australia, Europe, North America, and South America

Brazil is on the continent of South America.

equator /ɪˈkweɪtər/ *noun* the imaginary line around the middle of the Earth

Towns and cities near the equator are often very hot.

hemisphere /ˈhɛmɪˌsfir/ *noun* one of the halves of Earth, such as the northern or southern half

In the summer, the days are longer in the Northern Hemisphere.

pole /poʊl/ *noun* the most northern or southern point on Earth. These points are called the North Pole and the South Pole.

The explorers hiked over miles of ice before reaching the North Pole.

Write the word from above that describes each part of the globe below.

1. _____   _____

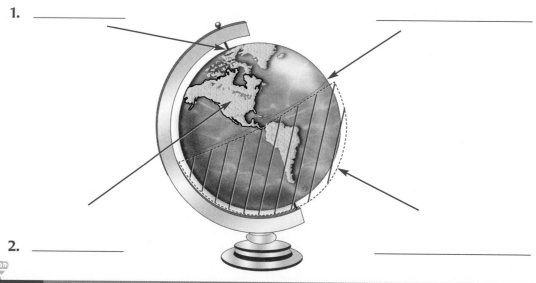

2. _____   _____

Write a paragraph about a trip. Pretend you traveled around the world. Where did you visit? What was it like there? Try to use one or more of the words above.

Tests with Word Maps

Some tests ask you to work with a drawing called a *word map*. In a word map, the word in the large oval in the center names a general category or group of things. The words around the oval name things in that group. The test asks you to choose a missing word for the word map. Remember that all the words around the oval are examples of the word in the oval.

Practice this strategy on these sample questions.

Directions: Read the words inside and outside the ovals. Find the missing words.

S1.   hamburger   bread   S2.   coat   shirt

         FOOD   ?

         ?   corn   dress   jeans

Ⓐ high   Ⓐ shoes

Ⓑ tree   Ⓑ clothes

Ⓒ soup   Ⓒ school

Ⓓ sound   Ⓓ grass

Does the word inside the oval name the things around it? The correct answers are on page 119.

Go on

PRACTICE TEST

Directions: Read the words inside and outside the ovals. Find the missing words.

1.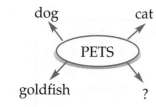
   dog   cat
   PETS
   goldfish   ?

   Ⓐ bird
   Ⓑ careful
   Ⓒ bicycle
   Ⓓ angry

2.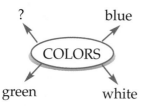
   ?   blue
   COLORS
   green   white

   Ⓐ rough
   Ⓑ book
   Ⓒ easy
   Ⓓ red

3.
   penny   quarter
   MONEY
   ?   dollar

   Ⓐ dime
   Ⓑ paper
   Ⓒ cost
   Ⓓ happy

4.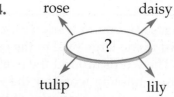
   rose   daisy
   ?
   tulip   lily

   Ⓐ flowers
   Ⓑ garden
   Ⓒ happy
   Ⓓ fat

5.
   May   July
   MONTHS
   ?   October

   Ⓐ Monday
   Ⓑ star
   Ⓒ January
   Ⓓ long

6.
   Mexico   China
   ?
   Cuba   United States

   Ⓐ oceans
   Ⓑ machines
   Ⓒ games
   Ⓓ countries

Correct answers are on page 119.

STOP

13

Slaves escape to the North using the Underground Railroad.

Harriet Tubman and the Underground Railroad

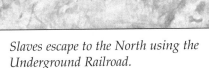

Reading Skill:
Using Context Clues

Expand Your Vocabulary:
Agriculture

Get Ready to Read

1. What is a slave? How is the life of a slave different from the life of a free person? List some differences below.

	Slaves	Free People
Work		*They can choose the work they do.*
Home		
Travel		

2. Look at the picture above and read the title of this chapter. What do you think an Underground Railroad is? What do you think you will learn about it in this reading selection?

_____

_____

🎧 Harriet Tubman and the Underground Railroad

1   Harriet Tubman was an African-American slave in Maryland on a plantation, which is a kind of large farm. But in 1849 after 30 years of hard work and cruel treatment, she was determined to be free or die trying. A white neighbor told her about the Underground Railroad. It was neither under the

5 ground nor a railroad. Instead it was the name for secret **routes** for slaves to escape to the North, where there was no slavery. One night, Tubman escaped to a house her neighbor told her about. The white people there told her to climb into a wagon and cover herself with straw. After several stops, Tubman reached the state of Pennsylvania. She was free. But Tubman was not **satisfied**

10 just to be free herself; she wanted to do more. She promised to return to the South to help other slaves escape.

    For two years, Tubman studied how the Underground Railroad worked. She learned about its **system** of barns, caves, and homes with hidden rooms where escaping slaves could hide. She saved money, bought some men's clothes, and

15 went back to the South. This was very dangerous. She knew that she could be made a slave again or even killed.

    But Tubman was brave and clever and avoided being caught. Once she got on a train going south. No one was likely to look for an escaped slave on a train going south. Another time she dropped some chickens she was holding.

20 Then she pretended to chase them until she was out of danger. Eventually she made at least seven trips back to

25 the plantation of her **former** owner, where she used to be a slave. Each time, she led groups of men, women,

30 and children out of slavery. One group included her parents. They waited their whole lives to be free.

Routes of the Underground Railroad around 1850

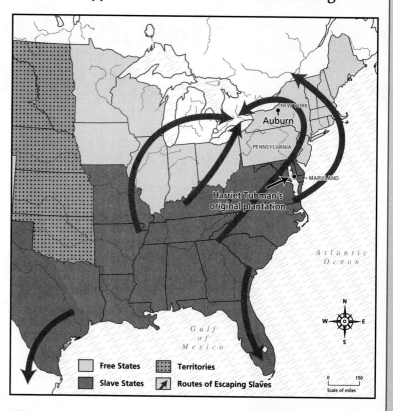

WANTED
HARRIET TUBMAN
$40,000

35 Slave owners **detested** Tubman and offered $40,000 for her capture. This was a very big amount of money at the time. However, the slaves respected her and called her Moses. According to the Bible, Moses led the Jewish people out of slavery in Egypt. In all, Tubman made 19 trips to the South and helped more than 300 slaves to escape.

45 Shortly after Tubman's last trip on the Underground Railroad, the Civil War began. Her work as a Union spy helped the North to win the war and **abolish** slavery, making all people in the 50 United States free. After the war, Tubman moved to a house in Auburn, New York. She died there in 1913. The Harriet Tubman house is still there today. Freedom Park opened nearby in 1994.

Harriet Tubman

Check Your Understanding

 1. Why did Tubman buy men's clothes before returning to the South?

_____

2. Why did Harriet Tubman once get on a train going south?

_____

3. How did Harriet Tubman help the North win the Civil War?

_____

What is the meaning of each word in blue? Fill in the correct bubble.

1. It was neither under the ground nor a railroad. Instead it was the name for secret **routes** for slaves to escape to the North, where there was no slavery.

   (A) written messages

   (B) ways to get from one place to another

   (C) rewards given to someone who captures a slave

   (D) laws that made slaves return to their owners

2. After several stops, Tubman reached the state of Pennsylvania. She was free. But Tubman was not **satisfied** just to be free herself; she wanted to do more. She promised to return to the South to help other slaves escape.

   (A) filled with hope

   (B) angry

   (C) happy about the way things are

   (D) able to understand

3. For two years, Tubman studied how the Underground Railroad worked. She learned about its **system** of barns, caves, and homes with hidden rooms where escaping slaves could hide.

   (A) group of parts that work together

   (B) confusing maps

   (C) materials needed to repair buildings

   (D) loud talk

4. Eventually she made at least seven trips back to the plantation of her **former** owner, where she used to be a slave. Each time, she led groups of men, women, and children out of slavery.

   (A) next

   (B) successful

   (C) lost

   (D) past

5. Slave owners **detested** Harriet Tubman and offered $40,000 for her capture. This was a very big amount of money at the time. However, the slaves respected her and called her Moses.

   (A) rewarded

   (B) hated

   (C) searched for

   (D) tricked

6. Her work as a Union spy helped the North to win the war and **abolish** slavery, making all people in the United States free.

   (A) get rid of

   (B) explain

   (C) make larger

   (D) move further away

Using Context Clues

When you don't know a word in a reading, use the words or sentences before and after it to help you guess its meaning. These words and sentences are called *context clues*. For example:

> the Underground Railroad... was neither under the ground nor a railroad. Instead it was the name for secret **routes** for slaves to escape to the North.

These sentences tell you that the Underground Railroad was a secret route and that slaves used it to travel to the North. So *routes* might be "ways to get from one place to another."

Work with a partner to find context clues in the reading for each word below and fill in the chart.

Vocabulary Word	Context Clues	What do the clues tell about the meaning of the vocabulary word?
routes	— *Underground Railroad... name for secret routes for slaves to escape to the North*	— *like a railroad, but not a railroad* — *Slaves used routes to escape.*
satisfied		
system		
former		
detested		
abolished		

Now look again at your answers to the vocabulary questions on page 88. Change any answers you think are wrong.

Agriculture

Read the definitions below of four words that are related to agriculture.

> **crop** /krɑp/ *noun* plants that are grown for food
>
> > *A large crop of corn will grow in this field.*
>
> **harvest** /ˈhɑrvəst/ *verb* to gather food plants from a field
>
> > *The farmers will harvest the corn soon.*
>
> **irrigate** /ˈɪrɪˌgeɪt/ *verb* to use pipes or ditches to bring water to a place such as a field
>
> > *After weeks with no rain, the farmer decided to irrigate his fields.*
>
> **soil** /sɔɪl/ *noun* the top layer of ground in which plants grow
>
> > *In the spring, I plant seeds deep in the soil.*

True or False? Use the definitions. Fill in the correct bubble.

		True	False
1.	Corn, wheat, and cabbage are different kinds of crops.	Ⓣ	Ⓕ
2.	Plants cannot grow in soil.	Ⓣ	Ⓕ
3.	Farmers usually harvest a crop before it produces food.	Ⓣ	Ⓕ
4.	If you irrigate a field, the soil gets wet.	Ⓣ	Ⓕ

Put It in Writing

Write a paragraph about crops that are grown where you live now or in another place you have lived. Try to use one or more of the words above.

Workers from the Central Pacific and Union Pacific Railroads meet at Promontory Point, Utah, on May 10, 1869.

A Railroad Unites a Nation

Reading Skill:
Separating Facts from Opinions

Expand Your Vocabulary:
Geography

Get Ready to Read

1. Building a railroad over mountains is not easy. Pretend you want to build a railroad. How will you solve the two problems below?

Problem	Possible Solution
Making a path through a mountain	• *Use explosions to make a hole through the mountain* •
Finding workers for this difficult and dangerous job	

2. Look at the picture above and the words under it. Read the title of this chapter. Write two questions you think this reading will answer.

_____

_____

🎧 A Railroad Unites a Nation

1   In 1850 going from the East Coast of the United States to the West Coast was difficult. The railroad ended halfway across the country. After that, there were only **rugged** trails and high mountains. Building a railroad to California was going to cost a lot of money. The railroad companies did not have the

5   money to do it. Some people said it was impossible to build a railroad over mountains. President Abraham Lincoln, however, thought building the railroad was **essential**. Without it, the United States could not grow. On July 1, 1862, Lincoln signed the Pacific Railroad Act. This law gave government money and land for the new railroad.

10   Two companies, the Union Pacific and the Central Pacific, were appointed to do the work. The Union Pacific began in Omaha, Nebraska, and started building toward the West. The Central Pacific began in Sacramento, California, and started building toward the East. When the two met, the East and West were going to be tied together.

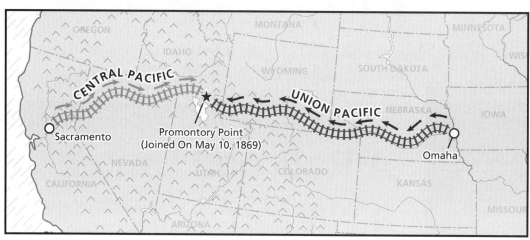

The route of the railroad from Omaha to Sacramento

15   The Central Pacific quickly **encountered** problems. The company needed 5,000 workers. It had only 600. After two years, only 50 miles of track were finished. The company still had the **enormous** task of crossing the mountains.

Someone suggested that the Central Pacific hire Chinese workers. The manager became angry and shouted that they were too small to do a "real

20   man's work." But an assistant answered, "Well, they did build the Great Wall of China." The manager changed his mind. At first, the Chinese workers were given unimportant jobs. They carried water or loaded wagons. Finally, they got the chance to do bigger jobs.

The Chinese men quickly proved that they were skillful workers. They

25 built more railroad track in less time than any of the **previous** teams. Soon, Chinese workers were doing the most difficult and **risky** jobs. They made the ground flat, carried iron rails, and swung heavy hammers. They even took the job of blasting a

30 path through the mountains. One worker was lowered on a rope over the side of a cliff. He then drilled a small hole in the cliff, filled it with blasting powder, and lit it. The others had to pull him up before the

35 powder exploded.

The Chinese were such good workers that they were chosen to finish the last ten miles of track. On May 10, 1869, in Promontory Point,

40 Utah, the two sets of track were joined with a golden spike. One hundred years later, a marker was placed on that spot to honor the Chinese workers. Their courage and

45 skill helped to unite a nation.

A hammer, rails, and spikes used to build th railroad

A team of Chinese workers who helped build the Central Pacific Railroad

Check Your Understanding

1. What two things did the Pacific Railroad Act give the railroad companies?

   _____

2. What were the names of the two railroad companies that built the railroad from Omaha to Sacramento?

   _____

3. Why were the Chinese workers first given only unimportant jobs?

   _____

   _____

What is the meaning of each word in blue? Fill in the correct bubble.

1. The railroad ended halfway across the country. After that, there were only **rugged** trails and high mountains.

   Ⓐ rough and uneven   Ⓒ hidden

   Ⓑ wide and smooth   Ⓓ dangerous

2. President Abraham Lincoln, however, thought building the railroad was **essential**. Without it, the United States could not grow.

   Ⓐ easy   Ⓒ too expensive

   Ⓑ dangerous   Ⓓ necessary

3. The Central Pacific quickly **encountered** problems. The company needed 5,000 workers. It had only 600.

   Ⓐ solved   Ⓒ avoided

   Ⓑ started having   Ⓓ delivered

4. After two years, only 50 miles of track were finished. The company still had the **enormous** task of crossing the mountains.

   Ⓐ unnecessary   Ⓒ simple

   Ⓑ finished   Ⓓ very big

5. The Chinese men quickly proved that they were skillful workers. They built more railroad track in less time than any of the **previous** teams.

   Ⓐ earlier   Ⓒ small

   Ⓑ well-trained   Ⓓ strong

6. Soon, Chinese workers were doing the most difficult and **risky** jobs. They made the ground flat, carried iron rails, and swung heavy hammers. They even took the job of blasting a path through the mountains.

   Ⓐ well-paid   Ⓒ dangerous

   Ⓑ fun   Ⓓ unimportant

Separating Facts from Opinions

A *fact* is something that you can prove. An *opinion* is someone's idea or belief that cannot be proved. You can agree or disagree with an opinion. Opinions often use words like *good, bad, best, worst,* and *too.*

> **Fact:** Lincoln signed the Pacific Railroad Act on July 1, 1862.
>
> **Opinion:** It's too much work to build a railroad over mountains.

Fact or Opinion? Fill in the correct bubble.

	Fact	Opinion
1. In the first two years, the Central Pacific finished only 50 miles of track.	Ⓕ	Ⓞ
2. The Union Pacific had the best workers.	Ⓕ	Ⓞ
3. The railroad was necessary for the country to expand.	Ⓕ	Ⓞ
4. The two rail lines were joined with a golden spike.	Ⓕ	Ⓞ
5. A Chinese work team finished the last ten miles of track.	Ⓕ	Ⓞ
6. Building the railroad to California cost too much money.	Ⓕ	Ⓞ
7. Blasting powder was used to clear a path through the mountains.	Ⓕ	Ⓞ
8. Using blasting powder to clear a path through the mountains was a good idea.	Ⓕ	Ⓞ

Geography

Read the definitions below of four kinds of land.

crevice /ˈkrɛvɪs/ *noun* a crack in a rock or mountain

The men squeezed through the narrow crevice.

plain /pleɪn/ *noun* a large, flat area of land, often with few trees

The wagons crossed the empty plain very quickly.

plateau /plæˈtoʊ/ *noun* a raised area of land with a flat top

From the plateau we could see for miles in every direction.

ridge /rɪdʒ/ *noun* a long narrow area of high land such as the top of a mountain

The sun set behind the ridge of the mountain.

Write the word from above that describes each picture.

1. _____

3. _____

2. _____

4. _____

Write a letter. Pretend you are a worker for the Central Pacific and tell someone about the work you did today. Try to use one or more of the words above.

Words with More Than One Meaning

Many words have more than one meaning. A dictionary gives each meaning and numbers it. The word *company* has four different meanings. Here is how this word might appear in a dictionary.

> **company** /ˈkʌmpəni/ *noun* (plural **companies**) **1** a guest or guests at your home **2** the situation of being with someone **3** a business **4** a unit of soldiers

Use the dictionary entry above to write the meaning of *company* in sentences 1–4.

1. I always enjoy the company of my friends from school.

_____

2. My father works for a company that makes bicycle parts.

_____

3. We are having company for dinner on Sunday.

_____

4. The captain led his company into the battle.

_____

Use the dictionary entry above to complete 5 and 6.

5. Write a sentence using the word company.

_____

_____

6. Write the meaning of *company* in the sentence you wrote.

_____

> **charge** /tʃɑrdʒ/ *verb* **charged, charging, charges 1** to ask for an amount
> of money as the price of something **2** to pay for something with a credit
> card **3** to attack a place with a lot of energy **4** to officially accuse or blame
> someone **5** to fill something with electrical energy

Study the dictionary entry for the verb *charge*. Then write **1, 2, 3, 4,** or **5** in the blanks
to show which meaning of *charge* is used in each sentence. The first one has been
done for you.

___2___ **1.** I didn't have much money with me, so I charged the purchase.

_____ **2.** The library charges 25 cents a day for books that are returned late.

_____ **3.** You need to charge the battery in your cell phone.

_____ **4.** The general's troops charged up the hill and captured the enemy.

_____ **5.** The police have not charged anyone with the crime.

_____ **6.** I just got the bill for the clothes I charged last month.

Each underlined word below has more than one meaning. Find each word in a
dictionary. Then write the meaning of the word used in the sentence.

7. I love to build <u>models</u> of airplanes and ships.

_____

8. A safety check of the car found that its <u>horn</u> was not working.

_____

9. The senator's <u>staff</u> answers her mail and greets visitors.

_____

10. Our <u>mission</u> was to save the whale that was caught in the fishing net.

_____

General Ulysses S. Grant accepts General Robert E. Lee's surrender at Appomattox, Virginia.

Surrender at Appomattox

Reading Skill:
Noticing Cause and Effect

Expand Your Vocabulary:
Ending Disagreements

Get Ready to Read

1. When you have a fight with a friend or family member, do you stay angry for a long time? What do you do to try to make the situation better after the fight is over?

   _____

   _____

2. Read the title and first paragraph of the reading selection on page 100. Write a sentence telling what you think this reading selection is about.

   _____

   _____

Surrender at Appomattox

1   From 1861 to 1865, Americans fought each other in a bloody war. The Confederate army fought for the Southern states. These states were trying to **secede** from the United States. They wanted to be a separate nation and keep their slaves. President Abraham Lincoln wanted to keep the North and the
5   South together and to free the slaves. The Union army from the North **supported** him.

     By 1865, the South was running out of men and supplies. The soldiers had few bullets and little food. In April 1865, General Robert E. Lee led his Confederate army out of Richmond, Virginia. General Ulysses S. Grant's large,
10   strong Union army was following them. Lee's officers wanted to lead their men to the mountains. They could hide there and make surprise attacks for years. Lee felt this was not honest or fair and **rejected** the idea.

     On the morning of April 9, 1865, Lee sent a message to Grant. Lee asked for a meeting to discuss the surrender of his army. Grant agreed to meet him in

15   a farmhouse near Appomattox, Virginia.

     Lee arrived early. He and his army expected to be Grant's prisoners by the end of the day. They might even be put on trial for **treason** and executed. A half-hour later, the Union officers arrived.

     Grant and Lee shook hands and talked pleasantly.
20   Although Grant's army defeated Lee and his army, Grant was not going to take away their **dignity**. The Southern soldiers agreed never to fight against the United States again, and Grant said they could go home. They were allowed to
25   keep their horses and mules. The animals were needed to plant spring crops.

     Lee thought Grant was very fair. However, he asked for one more thing: food. His men had little food for many days, and they were very hungry.
30   Grant told his officers to give Lee's troops food for 25,000 men.

     As Lee stepped outside, Union officers nearby stood up and saluted him. Lee saluted the **victorious** officers, got on his horse, and rode
35   away. When Union soldiers heard the news, they

A Union officer salutes General Lee.

began to cheer and shoot into the air. Grant ordered the celebrations to stop. He said that both armies were part of the same country again, and they should respect each other.

40 In 1864, the land around Lee's former home in Arlington, Virginia, was turned into a cemetery for soldiers. A Confederate and Union soldier were buried there, side by side. Today over 200,000 men and women who died for their country are buried in Arlington National Cemetery.

Grave markers in Arlington National Cemetery

Check Your Understanding

1. Why did Grant let the Confederate soldiers keep their horses and mules?

   _____

2. What favor did Lee ask Grant for after he surrendered?

   _____

 3. Why did Grant tell the soldiers to stop celebrating their victory?

   _____

What is the meaning of each word in blue? Fill in the correct bubble.

1. The Confederate army fought for the Southern states. These states were trying to **secede** from the United States. They wanted to be a separate nation and keep their slaves.

    (A) ask for help   (C) ask for money

    (B) choose   (D) officially leave

2. President Abraham Lincoln wanted to keep the North and the South together and to free the slaves. The Union army from the North **supported** him.

    (A) agreed with and helped   (C) fought against

    (B) disagreed with   (D) avoided

3. They could hide there and make surprise attacks for years. Lee felt this was not honest or fair and **rejected** the idea.

    (A) wrote down   (C) refused to accept

    (B) liked   (D) considered thoughtfully

4. He and his army expected to be Grant's prisoners by the end of the day. They might even be put on trial for **treason** and executed.

    (A) breaking a small law   (C) the crime of fighting against
                                       their own country

    (B) failing to feed their troops   (D) arriving early for a meeting

5. Although Grant's army defeated Lee and his army, Grant was not going to take away their **dignity**. The Southern soldiers agreed never to fight against the United States again, and Grant said they could go home.

    (A) tools needed for farming   (C) leaders in battle

    (B) respect   (D) weapons used in war

6. As Lee stepped outside, Union officers nearby stood up and saluted him. Lee saluted the **victorious** officers, got on his horse, and rode away.

    (A) strong   (C) frightening

    (B) angry   (D) winning

Noticing Cause and Effect

A *cause* is the reason something happens. An *effect* is the thing that happens.

> **Cause:** Lee's army had little food for many days.

> **Effect:** They were very hungry.

Words like *as a result, because, for that reason, so,* and *therefore* signal a cause and an effect.

Read each paragraph below. Then fill in the missing cause and effect in the chart.

On April 3, 1865, General Grant's army began entering the Confederate capital of Richmond. General Lee could not stop them, so he ordered his army out of the city. Grant knew it was dangerous to allow Lee's army to rest and get new supplies of food and bullets. Grant therefore ordered his troops to chase after them.

Cause	Effect
1. Grant's army entered Richmond.	
2.	Grant ordered his troops to chase Lee's army.

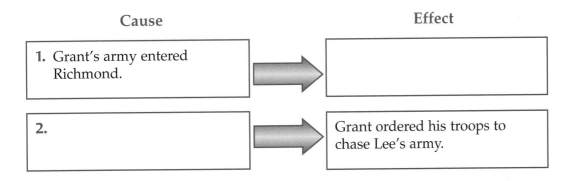

Lee could not get the food and bullets he needed, and his men were sick and tired. He decided to surrender because he knew he could not win. President Lincoln ordered Grant not to punish anyone in the defeated army. For that reason, Grant let Lee and his soldiers return to their homes and plant

Cause	Effect
3. Lee knew he could not win.	
4.	Grant let Lee and his soldiers return home.

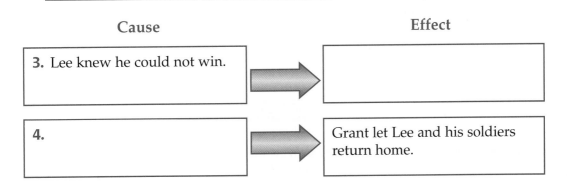

Ending Disagreements

Read the definitions below of four words that are related to ending disagreements.

compromise /ˈkɑmprəˌmaɪz/ *verb* to end a disagreement by making a deal in which everyone accepts less than they really want

Let's compromise—you ride the bike for an hour, and then I'll ride it.

conflict /ˈkɑnflɪkt/ *noun* a disagreement or fight between people, groups, or countries

The boss is trying to end the conflict between his two employees.

diplomatic /dɪpləˈmætɪk/ *adjective* careful about what you say so that you don't make someone else angry or upset

Susan is very diplomatic, so she gets along with everyone.

negotiate /nəˈgoʊʃiˌeɪt/ *verb* to talk to someone in order to try to end a disagreement

The two leaders are negotiating with each other to end the war.

Fill in each blank with the correct word from above.

Sometimes my friends and I do not agree about what we want to do. Then there

is a **(1)**_____ between us. I don't like to argue, so I try to

find a way to solve the problem. I have to be **(2)**_____

because I don't want my friends to get angry with me. We usually

(3)_____ for a while and explain our opinions. We finish

giving our reasons. Then we try to **(4)**_____. We do

some things that each person wants to do, but we don't do all of them.

Write a short newspaper story about Lee's surrender to Grant. Be sure your report answers the questions Who? What? Where? When? and Why? Try to use one or more of the words above.

John Wilkes Booth shoots President Abraham Lincoln in a balcony at Ford's theater.

Lincoln's Assassination

Get Ready to Read

1. List at least two things you know about Abraham Lincoln.

_____

_____

2. Look at the picture above and read the words under it. Write two questions you expect the reading to answer.

_____

_____

🎧 Lincoln's Assassination

1   Five days after the Civil War ended, on April 14, 1865, President Abraham Lincoln talked with his wife, Mary, about the sad things in their lives. Their son Willie was dead. The Civil War was finally over, but its effects were still very bad. Lincoln promised his wife that from now on life was going to be happier.

5   Lincoln thought that going to a comedy at Ford's Theater was a good start.

As the Lincolns prepared to go to the theater, the president's bodyguard asked if he should go with them. Lincoln **declined** his offer saying, "You've had a long hard day's work and must go home."

The Lincolns arrived late. As they went to their seats in the balcony, the
10   play stopped while the audience and the actors on the stage **applauded**. The Lincolns smiled. After several minutes, the play **resumed**. The audience loved the play. Everyone was laughing. But sometime during the play, John Wilkes Booth, a supporter of the defeated South, secretly entered the balcony with a gun. Then a gunshot made the crowd become silent. Seconds later, Booth
15   jumped from the balcony and landed on the stage. Lincoln was shot. Screams and confusion filled the theater.

A doctor in the audience had several men carry Lincoln to a house across the street. Lincoln's own doctor joined them there. After examining Lincoln's wound, both doctors agreed that Lincoln was not going to survive.

20   Meanwhile, there were other attempted **assassinations**. One man tried to kill the secretary of state. Fortunately, he failed. Another man was supposed to kill the vice
25   president, but he did not carry out the plan. Lincoln's murder seemed to be part of a **conspiracy**. Perhaps the South was starting the war
30   again. Edwin Stanton, the secretary of war, ordered troops to guard Washington, D.C. But there were no more attacks. Twelve days after the
35   assassination, John Wilkes Booth was

The Lincoln penny

trapped and killed on a farm in Virginia. The people who helped with the plan were caught, put on trial, and hanged.

40   Lincoln lived for nine hours after being shot. A train covered with black cloth carried his body back to Springfield, Illinois, the town he left four years earlier.

45 Millions of people watched and cried as the train passed.

    Today the Lincoln Memorial in Washington, D.C., contains a 19-foot, 175-ton statue of

50 Lincoln. The 36 columns of the building represent the 36 states in the country at the time of Lincoln's death. It is probably the best-known building in the nation. Its **image**, along with the image

55 of Lincoln, is found on millions of pennies.

The Lincoln Memorial on the back of the penny

Check Your Understanding

1. Why did Lincoln suggest going to a play?

    _____

2. What reason did Lincoln give for telling his bodyguard not to come with him to the theater?

    _____

3. How long did Lincoln live after he was shot?

    _____

What is the meaning of each word in blue? Fill in the correct bubble.

1. As the Lincolns prepared to go to the theater, the president's bodyguard asked if he should go with them. Lincoln **declined** his offer saying, "You've had a long hard day's work and must go home."

    - Ⓐ did not obey
    - Ⓑ laughed at
    - Ⓒ agreed
    - Ⓓ said no politely

2. The Lincolns arrived late. As they went to their seats in the balcony, the play stopped while the audience and the actors on the stage **applauded**. The Lincolns smiled.

    - Ⓐ clapped their hands
    - Ⓑ stopped and looked for a long time
    - Ⓒ became frightened
    - Ⓓ disappeared

3. As they went to their seats in the balcony, the play stopped while the audience and the actors on the stage applauded. The Lincolns smiled. After several minutes, the play **resumed**.

    - Ⓐ made people laugh
    - Ⓑ started from the beginning
    - Ⓒ ended
    - Ⓓ began again

4. Meanwhile, there were other attempted **assassinations**. One man tried to kill the secretary of state. Fortunately, he failed.

    - Ⓐ well-known plays
    - Ⓑ people who help others
    - Ⓒ murders of important people
    - Ⓓ crowded theaters

5. One man tried to kill the secretary of state. Fortunately, he failed. Another man was supposed to kill the vice president, but he did not carry out the plan. Lincoln's murder seemed to be part of a **conspiracy**.

    - Ⓐ secret plan by a group of people
    - Ⓑ government trick
    - Ⓒ war between nations
    - Ⓓ comedy

6. It is probably the best-known building in the nation. Its **image**, along with the image of Lincoln, is found on millions of pennies.

    - Ⓐ cover
    - Ⓑ picture
    - Ⓒ story
    - Ⓓ information

Making Inferences

You can sometimes use facts that are stated directly in a reading to guess certain facts that are not stated. This is called *making inferences*. Making inferences helps you understand more of what you read.

Stated Fact: The Lincolns arrived late. As they went to their seats, the play stopped while the audience and the actors on the stage applauded.

Inference: The people in the theater liked the Lincolns.

Fill in the bubble of the most likely inference that you can make from each of these stated facts.

1. Lincoln told his bodyguard he did not need to go to the theater with him.

   Ⓐ The bodyguard did not like plays.   Ⓒ There were no extra seats in the theater.

   Ⓑ Lincoln felt safe without his bodyguard   Ⓓ Lincoln did not like his bodyguard.

2. A doctor had men carry Lincoln to a house near the theater.

   Ⓐ The doctor lived in another city.   Ⓒ Lincoln was bleeding badly.

   Ⓑ The play was going to continue.   Ⓓ The doctor could treat Lincoln's wounds better in a house.

3. Booth jumped from the balcony where Lincoln was seated and landed on the stage.

   Ⓐ Booth was afraid of high places.   Ⓒ Lincoln was sitting near the stage.

   Ⓑ The theater was very small.   Ⓓ The actors were not on the stage.

4. A train carried Lincoln's body back to Springfield, Illinois, his hometown.

   Ⓐ Springfield, Illinois, is near Washington, D.C.   Ⓒ Lincoln is probably buried in Springfield, Illinois.

   Ⓑ The roads were not safe for travelers.   Ⓓ Trains were the only way to travel in 1865.

5. The Lincoln Memorial is familiar to most people because its picture is on pennies.

   Ⓐ Most people have seen a penny.   Ⓒ Pennies are not worth much.

   Ⓑ Many people visit Washington, D.C., each year.   Ⓓ We have pennies because of Lincoln.

The Theater

Read the definitions below of four words related to the theater.

> **plot** /plɑt/ *noun* the events that form the story in a play, movie, or book
>
> *The plot kept everyone interested for the entire movie.*
>
> **script** /skrɪpt/ *noun* the written words for actors in a play or movie
>
> *The actors studied the script for several hours before the performance.*
>
> **tragedy** /ˈtrædʒədi/ *noun* (plural **tragedies**) a serious play that ends sadly, usually with a death
>
> *The tragedy made the audience think about how suddenly life can change.*
>
> **villain** /ˈvɪlən/ *noun* the character in a play who fights against the hero
>
> *The audience cheered when the villain was caught.*

Fill in each blank with the correct word from above.

1. After the actor read the first page of the _____,
   she decided not to be in the play.

2. The _____ of the story was so confusing that no
   one could understand it.

3. In children's stories, the _____ is sometimes a
   wicked witch.

4. The _____ ends when the hero dies fighting to
   save his family.

Put It in Writing

Write a paragraph about a play or movie you have seen or a story you have read. Try to use one or more of the words above.

Tests with Posters, Signs, and Advertisements

Some tests ask you to work with a poster, sign, or advertisement. First read the questions. Then *scan* the entire poster, sign, or advertisement. In other words, let your eyes move quickly over all the information until you find the information you are looking for. Don't just read the information in large letters. Make sure to scan the information that is given with small letters and numbers too.

Practice this strategy on these sample questions.

Kwan saw this poster in his school library. He decided to go.

Take a Field Trip to the Science Museum!

All students are welcome to join Mr. Gill's science class.

- See a real Egyptian mummy!
- Learn why leaves change colors in the fall!
- Touch a moon rock!

The bus leaves Monday, at 9:00 a.m.
Sign up in the principal's office.
Bring a lunch.

S1. Where is Mr. Gill taking his class?
- Ⓐ to an art museum
- Ⓑ to the zoo
- Ⓒ to the science museum
- Ⓓ to the park

S2. What time does the bus leave?
- Ⓐ 9:00 a.m.
- Ⓑ 6:00 a.m.
- Ⓒ noon
- Ⓓ after school

S3. What must Kwan do in order to go?
- Ⓐ sign up in the principal's office
- Ⓑ buy a bus ticket
- Ⓒ see Mr. Gill
- Ⓓ go to the library

S4. Which of these will NOT be part of the field trip?
- Ⓐ seeing an Egyptian mummy
- Ⓑ touching a moon rock
- Ⓒ learning why leaves change color
- Ⓓ looking through a telescope

Did you scan all parts of the poster? Were you able to find the answers to the questions? The correct answers are on page 119.

Go on ▶

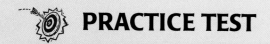 **PRACTICE TEST**

Pam saw this advertisement in a newspaper. She decided to visit the store.

Murphy's Department Store
112 Main Street

Giant Sale!

Shoes as cheap as $20!
All men's suits are half price!
Hats and gloves in all sizes and colors!

Pay by cash only. No checks, money orders, or credit cards.
Free parking behind the store.

Sale starts at eight o'clock Saturday morning and ends at midnight. All sales are final.
No purchases may be returned or exchanged.

---

1. What is the name of the store?
   A The Clothing Store
   B Murphy's Department Store
   C Main Street Store
   D Giant Sale!

2. What is the lowest price for shoes?
   A $10
   B $15
   C $20
   D $30

3. Where can Pam park free?
   A behind the store
   B on Main Street
   C a block away
   D in the city's parking lot

4. How can Pam pay for a hat?
   A check
   B money order
   C credit card
   D cash

5. Which of the following is NOT named in the advertisement?
   A shoes
   B hats
   C men's suits
   D coats

6. When does the sale begin?
   A 8:00 a.m.
   B midnight
   C noon
   D Monday

Correct answers are on page 119.

Glossary

Pronunciation Key									
Consonants						**Vowels**			
p	**p**ot	θ	**th**ing	h	**h**ot	i	b**ea**t	ʊ	b**oo**k
b	**b**all	ð	**th**at	m	**m**ap	ɪ	b**i**t	u	b**oo**t
t	**t**all	s	**s**ee	n	**n**ot	eɪ	l**a**te	ʌ	c**u**t
d	**d**og	z	**z**oo	ŋ	si**ng**	ε	l**e**t	ə	**a**bout
k	**c**at	ʃ	**sh**op	w	**w**ell	æ	p**a**t	ɜ	b**ir**d
g	**g**o	ʒ	mea**s**ure	r	**r**ide	ɑ	p**o**t	aɪ	wh**y**
f	**f**ine	tʃ	**ch**ip	l	**l**ook	ɔ	c**au**ght	aʊ	h**ow**
v	**v**oice	dʒ	**j**ump	j	**y**ou	oʊ	c**oa**t	ɔɪ	t**oy**

The symbol /ˈ/ before a syllable means that it is the main stressed syllable in a word.

The symbol /ˌ/ before a syllable means that it is the second-most important stressed syllable.

The **blue** numbers tell which chapter each word is taught in.

abandon /əˈbændən/ *verb* to leave someone or something **(1)**

abolish /əˈbɑlɪʃ/ *verb* to get rid of a law or a system **(13)**

accuse /əˈkjuz/ *verb* to say that you think someone has broken the law or done something wrong **(10)**

amateur /ˈæmətər/ *adjective* not very skillful **(8)**

anarchy /ˈænərki/ *noun* a situation in which there is no government or authority **(9)**

applaud /əˈplɔd/ *verb* to clap your hands **(16)**

appoint /əˈpɔint/ *verb* to pick someone for a job **(6)**

approval /əˈpruvəl/ *noun* official permission to do something **(4)**

assassination /əˌsæsɪˈneɪʃən/ *noun* a murder of an important person **(16)**

assault /əˈsɔlt/ *noun* an attack **(9)**

assemble /əˈsɛmbəl/ *verb* to put something together **(7)**

authority /əˈθɔrəti/ *noun* power and control **(9)**

autobiography /ˌɔtoʊbaɪˈɑgrəfi/ *noun* the story of someone's life written by that person **(8)**

ballot /ˈbælət/ *noun* a piece of paper on which someone marks his or her vote **(5)**

barrier /ˈbæriər/ *noun* something that blocks your way and stops you from going somewhere **(7)**

biography /baɪˈɑgrəfi/ *noun* the story of someone's life written by another person **(8)**

campaign /kæmˈpeɪn/ *noun* a set of actions in order to achieve something **(11)**

canal /kəˈnæl/ *noun* an artificial river for ships **(2)**

candidate /ˈkændɪˌdeɪt/ *noun* a person who is trying to be elected to a government job **(5)**

canyon /ˈkænjən/ *noun* a narrow area of low land between steep cliffs **(7)**

capital /ˈkæpɪtəl/ *noun* the city where the government is **(6)**

capture /ˈkæptʃər/ *verb* to take someone as prisoner **(7)**

career /kəˈrir/ *noun* someone's job or profession for a long time **(6)**

challenge /ˈtʃæləndʒ/ *verb* to officially ask if a law is legal **(10)**

citizen /ˈsɪtɪzən/ *noun* a legal member of a particular country **(5)**

colonist /ˈkɑlənɪst/ *noun* a person who lives in a colony **(4)**

colony /ˈkɑləni/ *noun* an area that is controlled by a more powerful country **(3)**

complex /kɑmˈplɛks/ *adjective* made up of many small details **(6)**

compromise /ˈkɑmprəˌmaɪz/ *verb* to end a disagreement by making a deal in which everyone accepts less than they really want (15)

conflict /ˈkɑnflɪkt/ *noun* a disagreement or fight between people, groups, or countries (15)

Congress /ˈkɑŋgrəs/ *noun* the branch of the U.S. government that votes on laws for the president to approve (6)

consipracy /kənˈspɪrəsi/ *noun* a secret plan by a group of people (16)

continent /ˈkɑntɪnənt/ *noun* one of the seven large land areas of the Earth (12)

courageous /kəˈreɪdʒəs/ *adjective* brave and willing to do dangerous things (7)

crevice /ˈkrɛvɪs/ *noun* a narrow crack in a rock or mountain (14)

crop /krɑp/ *noun* plants that are grown for food (13)

cruel /ˈkruəl/ *adjective* mean and willing to hurt other people (2)

current /ˈkɜrənt/ *noun* a movement of water (2)

customer /ˈkʌstəmər/ *noun* a person who buys goods or services from a store (3)

debate /dɪˈbeɪt/ *noun* an argument or discussion (5)

decline /dɪˈklaɪn/ *verb* to say no politely to an offer (16)

defeat /dɪˈfit/ *verb* to win against or beat someone (5)

defendant /dɪˈfɛndənt/ *noun* a person who is being judged in a court of law (10)

democracy /dɪˈmɑkrəsi/ *noun* a system in which the people can vote to choose the people in their government (9)

depart /dɪˈpɑrt/ *verb* to leave a place (12)

desert /ˈdɛzərt/ *noun* a dry area often covered with sand with few plants (7)

determine /dɪˈtɜrmɪnd/ *adjective* wanting to do something very much (8)

detest /dɪˈtɛst/ *verb* hate (13)

dictatorship /dɪkˈteɪtərˌʃɪp/ *noun* government by one person with complete power (9)

dignity /ˈdɪgnəti/ *noun* respect (15)

diplomatic /dɪpləˈmætɪk/ *adjective* careful about what you say so that you don't make someone else angry or upset (15)

dispute /dɪsˈpjut/ *noun* an argument (9)

distrubute /dɪsˈstrɪˈbjut/ *verb* to give something to a large number of people (8)

document /ˈdɑkjəmənt/ *noun* an important paper (5)

doubt /daʊt/ *verb* to think that something is probably not true (12)

drought /draʊt/ *noun* a long period of time without rain (1)

employee /ɪmˈplɔɪi/ *noun* a person who is paid to work for another person or company (3)

employer /ɪmˈplɔɪər/ *noun* a person or business that pays someone to do work (3)

encounter /ɪnˈkaʊntər/ *verb* to start having problems when you are trying to do something (14)

enormous /ɪˈnɔrməs/ *adjective* very big (14)

equator /ɪˈkweɪtər/ *noun* the imaginary line around the middle of the Earth (12)

essential /ɪˈsɛntʃəl/ *adjective* necessary (14)

eventually /ɪˈvɛntʃəli/ *adverb* in the end, after a process or period of time (11)

evidence /ˈɛvɪdəns/ *noun* facts or objects that prove something (1)

expand /ɪkˈspænd/ *verb* to make something larger (11)

feud /fjud/ *noun* a disagreement or strong dislike between people or groups (4)

fever /ˈfivər/ *noun* a higher than normal body temperature when you are sick (11)

fiction /ˈfɪkʃən/ *noun* books or stories that are invented or made up (8)

flood /flʌd/ *noun* a lot of extra water that covers land that is usually dry (1)

former /ˈfɔrmər/ *adjective* in the past but not anymore (13)

foundation /faʊnˈdeɪʃən/ *noun* a basic belief or fact (5)

gulf /gʌlf/ *noun* a large area of ocean that is partly surrounded by land (2)

harvest /ˈhɑrvəst/ *verb* to gather food plants from a field (13)

hemisphere /ˈhɛmɪˌsfɪr/ *noun* one of the halves of Earth, such as the northern or southern half (12)

hostile /ˈhɑstəl/ *adjective* angry and very unfriendly (4)

House of Representitives /ˌhaʊs əv rɛprɪˈsɛntətɪvz/ *noun* the larger of the two parts of Congress. States with more people have more representatives. **(6)**

hurricane /ˈhɜrɪˌkeɪn/ *noun* a very large tropical storm with heavy rain and strong winds **(1)**

identical /aɪˈdɛntɪkəl/ *adjective* exactly the same **(6)**

image /ˈɪmədʒ/ *noun* a picture **(16)**

infection /ɪnˈfɛkʃən/ *noun* an illness caused by bacteria or a virus that attacks your body **(11)**

influence /ˈɪnfluəns/ *noun* an ability to change things **(12)**

inhabitant /ɪnˈhæbɪtənt/ *noun* a person who lives somewhere **(1)**

instrument /ˈɪnstrəmənt/ *noun* a tool that is used for scientific work **(6)**

investor /ɪnˈvɛstər/ *noun* a person who uses his or her money to form a business **(3)**

irrigate /ˈɪrɪˌgeɪt/ *verb* to use pipes or ditches to bring water to a place such as a field **(13)**

issue /ˈɪʃu/ *noun* a subject that people disagree about **(5)**

jealous /ˈdʒɛləs/ *adjective* unhappy because you want what someone else has **(3)**

journey /ˈdʒɜrni/ *noun* a long trip **(7)**

jury /ˈdʒɜri/ *noun* a group of citizens who are chosen to watch a trial and decide if someone is guilty or not guilty **(10)**

legend /ˈlɛdʒənd/ *noun* a story told for many years **(10)**

legislature /ˈlɛdʒɪˌsleɪtʃər/ *noun* people elected to make laws **(11)**

loyalty /ˈlɔjəlti/ *noun* love and support **(9)**

lumber /ˈlʌmbər/ *noun* wood used for building **(12)**

majority /məˈdʒɔrəti/ *noun* more than half **(10)**

militia /məˈlɪʃə/ *noun* an army made up of people who are not regular soldiers but fight in an emergency **(4)**

monarchy /ˈmɑnərki/ *noun* government by a king or queen **(9)**

negotiate /nəˈgoʊʃiˌeɪt/ *verb* to talk to someone in order to try to end a disagreement **(15)**

nonfiction /nɑnˈfɪkʃən/ *noun* books or articles about facts or real events **(8)**

nutritious /nuˈtrɪʃəs/ *adjective* healthy and good for your body **(7)**

oppose /əˈpoʊz/ *verb* to not agree with something and try to stop or change it **(10)**

order /ˈɔrdər/ *verb* to officially tell someone to do something **(2)**

patriotic /ˌpeɪtriˈɑtɪk/ *adjective* showing love for your country **(8)**

peninsula /pəˈnɪnsələ/ *noun* a piece of land that sticks out into an area of water **(2)**

permanent /ˈpɜrmənənt/ *adjective* lasting forever **(2)**

plain /pleɪn/ *noun* a large, flat area of land, often with few trees **(14)**

plateau /plæˈtoʊ/ *noun* a raised area of land with a flat top **(14)**

plot /plɑt/ *noun* the events that form the story in a play, movie, or book **(16)**

pole /poʊl/ *noun* the most northern or southern point on Earth **(12)**

population /ˌpɑpjəˈleɪʃən/ *noun* the number of people living in a place **(12)**

prairie /ˈprɛri/ *noun* a wide area of flat land covered with grass but few trees **(7)**

precise /prɪˈsaɪs/ *adjective* exact and correct **(11)**

preserve /prɪˈzɜrv/ *verb* to protect and keep something **(1)**

previous /ˈpriviəs/ *adjective* earlier or happening before **(14)**

principle /ˈprɪnsəpəl/ *noun* an idea about what is right and wrong **(5)**

profit /ˈprɑfɪt/ *noun* money that a business makes **(3)**

prosperous /ˈprɑspərəs/ *adjective* good at making money **(3)**

purchase /ˈpɜrtʃəs/ *verb* to buy something **(3)**

radical /ˈrædikəl/ *adjective* completely new and different **(11)**

ratify /ˈrætəˌfaɪ/ *verb* to make an agreement legal and official **(10)**

rebellion /rɪˈbɛljən/ *noun* a war that you fight against your government **(4)**

refuse /rɪˈfjuz/ *verb* to say no to doing something **(10)**

reject /rɪˈdʒɛkt/ *verb* to refuse to accept something **(15)**

release /rɪˈlis/ *verb* to let a prisoner go **(8)**

remote /rɪ'moʊt/ *adjective* far away (1)

representative /rɛprɪ'zɛntətɪv/ *noun* a person who is elected to speak for others (5)

resume /rɪ'zum/ *verb* to begin doing something again (16)

revenge /rɪ'vɛndʒ/ *noun* an action to punish someone for hurting you (9)

ridge /rɪdʒ/ *noun* a long narrow area of high land such as the top of a mountain (14)

risky /'rɪski/ *adjective* dangerous (14)

route /rut/ *noun* a way to get from one place to another (13)

rugged /'rʌgəd/ *adjective* rough and uneven (14)

rumor /'rumər/ *noun* a story that may not be true (2)

satisfied /'sætɪsˌfaɪd/ *adjective* happy about the way things are (13)

script /skrɪpt/ *noun* the written words for actors in a play or movie (16)

secede /sɪ'sid/ *verb* to officially take part of a country away from the rest (15)

seize /siz/ *verb* to take by force (4)

Senate /'sɛnət/ *noun* the smaller of the two parts of Congress. Each state elects two senators. (6)

settle /'sɛtəl/ *verb* to start living somewhere for a long time (1)

soil /sɔɪl/ *noun* the top layer of ground in which plants grow (13)

support /sə'pɔrt/ *verb* to agree with and help someone (15)

Supreme Court /səˌprim 'kɔrt/ *noun* the court of law in the U.S. with authority over all other courts (6)

surrender /sə'rɛndər/ *verb* to give up when you are fighting (8)

survivior /sər'vaɪvər/ *noun* a person who is still alive after something happens (9)

suspicious /sə'spɪʃəs/ *adjective* believing that something unusual or unexpected might in fact be true (12)

system /'sɪstəm/ *noun* a group of parts that work together (13)

tension /'tɛnʃən/ *noun* unfriendly feelings and anger (4)

therapy /'θɛrəpi/ *noun* an activity used to heal an injury or cure an illness (11)

tornado /tɔr'neɪdoʊ/ *noun* a violent storm with strong wind that often comes down from one cloud (1)

tragedy /'trædʒədi/ *noun* a serious play that ends sadly, usually with a death (16)

treason /'trizən/ *noun* the crime of fighting against your own country (15)

treasure /'trɛʒər/ *noun* something that is worth a lot of money (2)

treaty /'triti/ *noun* an agreement between two or more countries (4)

trial /'traɪəl/ *noun* a legal process in which a court of law decides if someone is guilty or not guilty (10)

vaccinate /'væksɪˌneɪt/ *verb* to put a substance into someone's body in order to protect the person from getting a disease (11)

valley /'væli/ *noun* a low area of land between two mountains or hills (7)

victorious /vɪk'tɔriəs/ *adjective* winning (15)

villain /'vɪlən/ *noun* the character in a play who fights against the hero (16)

wages /'weɪdʒəs/ *noun* [plural] money given to a worker for work he or she has done (3)

wetland /'wɛtˌlænd/ *noun* an area of land that is usually covered by water (2)

wounded /'wundɪd/ *adjective* hurt or injured (4)

READING

Comprehension

factual: 3, 9, 17, 23, 27, 28, 31, 37, 45, 51, 59, 65, 73, 79, 87, 93, 101, 107
inferential: 3, 9, 11, 17, 23, 28, 31, 37, 45, 51, 59, 65, 73, 79, 87, 93, 101, 107
main idea: 61, 75

Critical Thinking

1, 3, 6, 7, 9, 15, 17, 19, 21, 23, 25, 29, 35, 37, 40, 43, 45, 48, 49, 51, 53, 54, 57, 59, 62, 63, 65, 68, 71, 73, 76, 77, 79, 81, 82, 85, 87, 91, 93, 96, 99, 101, 105, 107, 109, 110

Literary Content

8000 B.C.–1200 A.D.: Pre-Columbian Americans: 1
1513–1565: Spanish exploration of Florida: 7
1621–1664: New Amsterdam: 15
1775: American Revolution: 21
1776–1783: Declaration of Independence: 29
1753–1792: Banneker's role in design of Washington, D.C.: 35
1804–1805: Sacagawea/Lewis and Clark: 43
1814: Writing of U.S. national anthem: 49
1836–1845: Texas War of Independence: 57
1830–1839: Displacement of Native Americans: 63
1841–1880: Care of mentally ill: 71
1847–1850: Gold rush in California: 77
1840–1865: Underground Railroad: 85
1862–1869: Chinese workers/Central Pacific Railroad: 91
1865: Lee's surrender to Grant: 99
1865: Lincoln's assassination: 105

Skills

asking yourself questions: 25
finding supporting details: 75
making inferences: 81
making a personal connection: 53
noticing cause and effect: 39, 103
noticing sequence of events: 33, 47
previewing: xiv, 5
reading continuous prose: 2–3, 8–9, 16–17, 22–23, 27, 30–31, 36–37, 44–45, 50–51, 58–59, 64–65, 72–73, 78–79, 86–87, 92–93, 100–101, 106–107
separating facts from opinions: 95
scanning: 111–112
skimming: 5, 27–28
using context clues: 11, 89
visualizing: 19

Pre-reading Questions

1, 7, 15, 21, 29, 35, 43, 49, 57, 63, 71, 77, 85, 91, 99, 105

Reading Through Art

1, 3, 6, 7, 9, 12, 15, 16, 17, 20, 21, 28, 29, 31, 34, 35, 37, 43, 45, 48, 49, 50, 51, 54, 57, 59, 62, 63, 65, 71, 72, 78, 82, 85, 87, 91, 93, 96, 99, 100, 101, 106, 107, 112

Reading Through Maps

2, 8, 12, 16, 22, 36, 44, 48, 58, 64, 79, 86, 92

Test-Taking Strategies

reading comprehension tests: 27–28
tests with posters, signs, and advertising: 111–112
tests with word maps: 83–84
vocabulary tests: 55–56

VOCABULARY

building of: 4, 10, 18, 24, 32, 38, 40, 46, 52, 60, 66, 74, 80, 88, 94, 101, 108
expansion of: 6, 12, 20, 26, 34, 40, 48, 54, 62, 68, 76, 82, 90, 96, 104, 110
glossary: 113–116

Academic Vocabulary

agriculture: 90
courts of law: 68
ending disagreements: 104
geography: 12, 48, 82, 96
government: 34, 40, 68
health: 76
literature: 54
peace and war: 26
the theater: 110
weather: 6
work and workers: 20

WORKSHOPS

I: Word Power: The Dictionary: 13–14
II: Test-Taking Strategies: Reading Comprehension Tests (Skimming): 27
   Practice Test: 28
III: Word Power: Prefixes and Suffixes: 41–42
IV: Test-Taking Strategies: Vocabulary Tests: 55
   Practice Test: 56
V: Word Power: Homophones: 69–70
VI: Tests with Word Maps: 83
   Practice Test: 84

WRITING

Answer Key to Test-Taking Workshops

Workshop II (pages 27–28)

S.	D
1.	B
2.	D
3.	C
4.	A

Workshop VI (pages 83–84)

S1.	C
S2.	B
1.	A
2.	D
3.	A
4.	A
5.	C
6.	D

Workshop IV (pages 55–56)

S1.	A
S2.	D
S3.	A
S4.	D
1.	A
2.	B
3.	B
4.	D
5.	A
6.	B
7.	C
8.	A

Workshop VIII (pages 111–112)

S1.	C
S2.	A
S3.	A
S4.	D
1.	B
2.	C
3.	A
4.	D
5.	D
6.	A